A Travel Guide to
American History

By
DAVE SWEENEY

Available as digital Ebook

ISBN 978-1-960903-70-9 (paperback)

Copyright © 2021 by Dave Sweeney. 833572

All rights reserved. No part of this book may

be reproduced or transmitted in any form or by any means, electronic or mechanical, including photocopying, recording, or by any information storage and retrieval system, without permission writing from the copyright owner.

Rev. date: 01/16/24

Publify Publishing

1412 W. Ave B

Lampasas, TX 76550

publifypublishing@gmail.com

American history, knowing the story of us. Men and women of pure grit and courage have made America what she is today. My guide will show you places in each state where history was made. These are places I have visited myself. I have visited Washington, DC, which in itself, a historical place. This is a small portion of history that is out there for you to see, enjoy, and learn about America. America is a nation founded on Christian principles and is blessed by God. "One nation, indivisible, with liberty and justice for all". My hope is as you travel America is that my book will guide you to some fantastic sites of history. My prayer, is every family, would use my book to teach their children at home. Our children need to know our history, which they are not being taught in our schools today.

This book is dedicated to all my Vietnam Brothers

CONTENTS

ALABAMA 1

ARIZONA 4

ARKANSAS 7

CALIFORNIA 9

COLORADO 12

CONNECTICUT 15

DELAWARE 16

FLORIDA 18

GEORGIA 20

HAWAII 23

IDAHO 24

ILLINOIS 25

INDIANA 27

IOWA 30

KANSAS 31

KENTUCKY 33

LOUISIANA 35

MARYLAND 37

MASSACHUSETTS 40

MICHIGAN 42

MINNESOTA 43

MISSISSIPPI 44

MISSOURI 47

MONTANA 49

NEBRASKA 51

NEVADA 52

NEW JERSEY 54

NEW MEXICO 55

NEW YORK 56

NORTH CAROLINA 58

NORTH DAKOTA	60
OHIO	61
OKLAHOMA	64
OREGON	66
PENNSYLVANIA	67
SOUTH CAROLINA	71
SOUTH DAKOTA	75
TENNESSEE	77
TEXAS	80
UTAH	85
VIRGINIA	86
WASHINGTON	94
WEST VIRGINIA	95
WISCONSIN	100
WYOMING	101

ALABAMA

USS Alabama is a retired battleship docked at Battleship Memorial Park in Mobile, AL. Commissioned 1942, saw action in the Pacific. USS Drum Submarine is also docked there was first sub completed and first to enter WWII. It's the only sub of her class in existence.

Ft. Gaines - Dauphin, AL.

Established 1821. Known for battle of Mobile Bay. Huge Anchor from USS Hartford, Admiral Farragut Flagship. He commanded from this ship "Damn the torpedoes, full speed ahead". Can view ships keel section washed ashore by Hurricane George 1998.

Ft. Mims - 30 miles North of Mobile

Massacre occurred 1813. Creek War, when a force of Creek Indians, members of Red Sticks Faction stormed the Fort. 500 died during the massacre.

Ten Oaks - 805 Pelham Rd. Jacksonville, AL.

Built in 1856 and used as headquarters for Gen. P.G.T. Beauregard

Ft. Morgan - 23 miles West of Gulf Shores - Hwy 180

Built between 1819 and 1833. Played significant role in battle of Mobile Bay, 1864. Used till 1946. Named for one of the least known generals of the Revolutionary War, Daniel Morgan.

Tuskegee Airman National Historic Site - Tuskegee, AL.

Built in 1940. In 1941 the All Black Pursuit Squadron was based here. "Tuskegee Experiment" the Army Air Corps Program to train African Americans to fly. They flew 1,578 missions, shot down 112 enemy aircraft. Moton Field was the primary training center.

Horseshoe Bend Military Park - Near Alexander City, AL.

Site of the last battle of the Creek War March 27, 1814

Andrew Jackson won a decisive victory against the Red Stick Nation. Over 800 Creeks died.

U.S. Space & Rocket Center I-65 Huntsville, AL.

This is the place if you want to learn about space. Over 1500 artifacts.

First White House of Confederacy

Located in Montgomery at 644 Washington Av. Built in 1835. Was residence of President Jefferson Davis and his family. Completely furnished.

ARIZONA

Yuma Territorial Prison - 220 Prison Hill Rd. - Yuma, AZ.
Opened in 1876 and closed 1909. 3,069 prisoners served here, 29 being women.

Apache Pass - Near Ft. Bowie
In 1857, the government awarded John Butterfield a contract to carry mail by stagecoach for over 2 yrs. The Chiricahuas allowed stages safe passage in exchange for gifts.

Ft. Bowie - Near Willcox, AZ.
Built 1864 Fort was built after battle of Apache Pass.

Named after Colonel George Washington Bowie who first established the Fort.

Geronimo Surrender Monument - Hwy 80 East of Douglas

Surrendered to Lt. Charles Gatewood in 1886. He died 1909 in Ft. Sill Hospital as a Prisoner of War.

Ft. Apache - Ft. Apache Indian Reservation

Army Post from 1870-1924 Built to control Apaches

Cochise Stronghold - Coronado National Forest

Natural fortress and hideout for Apache Indians of the Chiricahua Tribe led by Cochise. It is believed that Cochise was buried somewhere in the Stronghold. His friend Tom Jeffords knows the site. It died with him.

Tombstone - Hwy 80

"The town too tough to die"

Founded in 1877 by Prospector Ed Schieffelin

Meteor Crater - 18 miles West of Winslow, AZ.

50,000 yrs. old. During the 1960's and 70's NASA trained for missions to the moon.

ARKANSAS

Louisiana Purchase State Park - Hwy 362 near Blackton, AR.

United States and French Empire signed agreement on April 30, 1803. 830,000 square miles of land west of the Mississippi River, doubling the size of America.

Pea Ridge Military Park

15930 East US62 Garfield, AR.

Battle fought March 7-8, 1862, and saved Missouri for the Union.

Hope - William Clinton Birthplace Home - 117 S. Hervey St.

Bill Clinton, the 42nd President of the United States, spent the first 4 yrs. of his life. Born Aug. 19, 1946

Ft. Smith - Located on Oklahoma Border

Most noted for Judge Isaac Parker, the hanging judge More men were put to death by the U.S. government, than in any other place in American history.

Maintain law & order for over 80 yrs at Ft. Smith.

Judge Parker sentenced over 150 people to death, with no appeal.

Ft. Chaffee - Adjacent to Ft. Smith.

In 1958 Elvis Presley spent 4 days here as part of his induction into the Army. Building 803 is where he received his military haircut. See letter written to Pres. Eisenhower, by several ladies, requesting that they would not shave his head.

Sam Walton - First Walmart Store - 105 N. Main St. Bentonville

Walton started his business 1945 with $5,000 of his own money and a loan of $20,000

CALIFORNIA

Simi Valley - Ronald Reagan Library
40 Presidential Dr.

40th President of the United States and burial place of
President Reagan and First Lady Nancy Reagan

Chiriaco Summit, CA. George S. Patton Museum
62510 Chiriaco Rd.

Large collection of vehicles used during WWII and Korea

Plenty of memorabilia from Patton's life.

Sacramento, CA. - Sutters Fort - 2701 "L" Street

Established in 1839 owned by John Sutter. Fort was abandoned in 1848 after the discovery of gold at Sutters Mill in Coloma also owned by John Sutter.

Truckee, CA. - Donner Memorial - 12593 Donner Pass Rd.

Legendary pioneers who were victims of the harsh Sierra Nevada Winter of 1846 to 1847. Party of 90 emigrants headed to California. Only half survived.

San Francisco - Alcatraz Military Prison

Federal Prison from 1934 till 1963. Cold water and strong current made escape impossible.

Manzanar - Relocation Center - Manzanar Reward Rd.

Site of Concentration Camp where more than 120,000

Japanese Americans were held from 1942-1945

Eureka, CA. - Fort Humboldt Historic Park - 3431 Fort Av.

Operational from 1853-1870. Can see functional steam donkey engine and authentic native American dug-out canoe. Ulysses S. Grant served here for 5 months as a captain.

San Francisco - Fort Point Historic Site - 201 Marine Dr.

Located on south side of Golden Gate Bridge

Built in 1861 to defend San Francisco Bay from hostile warships.

Colma - Hills of Eternity Cemetery - 1301 El Camino Real

Final resting place of Wyatt Earp and Josephine Earp. In all his years of law, Wyatt was never grazed by a bullet.

COLORADO

Telluride, Co. - Butch Cassidy's First Bank Robbery Site now sells sunglasses. 129/131 W. Colorado Av. Mahr Building

Boulder, Co. - Grave of Tom Horn - Columbia Cemetery
9th & Pleasant Streets

Horn was a Pinkerton agent and a hired gun. Believed to have killed 17 as a hired gun. Convicted 1902 of killing a 14 year old boy. His tombstone is red an sits low.

Golden, Co. - Lookout Mountain Park

987 Lookout Mountain Rd. Burial Site of "Buffalo Bill" Cody.

Durango, Co. - Durango & Silverton Railroad.

The line between these towns

has run continuously since 1881. Train was robbed by Butch and Sundance

Cortez, Co. - Mesa Verde National Park

Largest Archaeological Preserve in the United States starting about 7500 BC.

Glenwood Springs, Co. - Grave of Doc Holliday - 732 Grand Av.

Holliday died from tuberculosis in 1887. He was 36. ½ mile hike up trail to grave in Linwood Cemetery.

CONNECTICUT

Coventry, CT. - Nathan Hale Home - 2299 South St.

Hale was an American patriot, soldier, and spy for Washington's

Army. He was captured & executed.

Wethersfield, CT. - Joseph Webb House - 211 Main St.

George Washington and Rochambeau a French General planned the campaign ending at Yorktown 1781

New Haven, CT. - Louis Lunch - 261 Crown St.

Lunch spot which claims to have served 1st hamburger

Danbury, CT. - Sybil Ludington Statue - 170 Main St.

Heroine of the American Revolutionary War. April 26, 1777, at age 16, she made an all-night ride by horse to alert American Forces of approaching British Forces.

DELAWARE

New Castle, DE. - Court House - 211 Delaware St.

Built in 1732. Here in 1776 New Castle, Kent, and Sussex counties declared Independence from England.

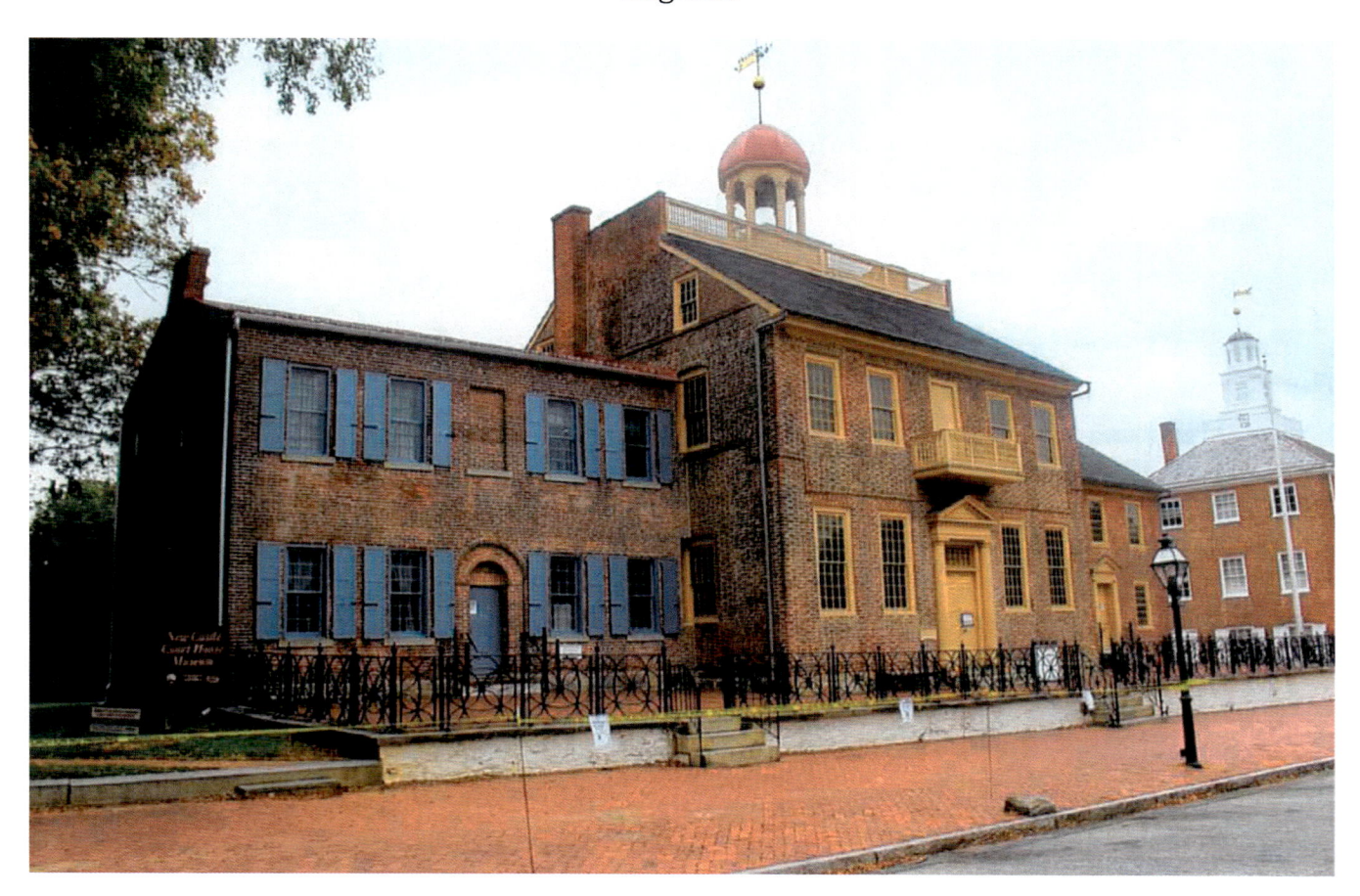

New Castle, DE. - Packet Alley - 25 Strand

Through this alley passed Andrew Jackson, David Crockett, Daniel Webster, Henry Clay, Sam Houston, Stonewall Jackson on their way to and from Washington, DC. Stagecoaches on one end and riverboats on the other.

New Castle, DE. - George Read House - 42 The Strand

Built in 1797-1804. Read was a lawyer, the son of one of the founding fathers. Ran several times for high office but was defeated each time.

New Castle, DE. - New Castle and Frenchtown Railroad

Built in 1832, one of the first railroads in the country

FLORIDA

Merritt Island, FL. - Kennedy Space Center

From the beginning to current space missions on display here.

Titusville, FL. - Warbird Museum - 6600 Tico Rd.

Maintains and restores aircraft from pre-WWI to the present. Over 45 historic warbirds.

St. Augustine, FL. - Castillo de San Marcos - 1 S Castillo Dr.

The oldest masonry fort in the United States. Construction began in 1672

Pensacola Beach, FL. - Fort Pickens - 1400 Fort. Pickens Rd.

Fort. was completed in 1834 and named after Andrew Pickens an American Revolutionary War militia leader. Fort remained in Union hands throughout the Civil War.

Key West, FL. - Ft. Jefferson - Dry Tortugas National Park

Fort is largest brick masonry structure in the Americas, with over 16 million bricks. Dr. Mudd did time here for giving medical care to John Wilkes Booth.

Sarasota, FL - Navy/Wac Kissing Statue Sarasota Bay Front 26 ft.

"Unconditional Surrender" Statue modeled after kissing scene in Times Square at the end of WW II.

GEORGIA

Savannah, GA. - Fort Pulaski National Monument - US 80

During the Civil War, the Union Army tested rifled cannon here in 1862. Also a P.O.W. Camp. Named for General Casimir Pulaski. Fort was completed in 1847.

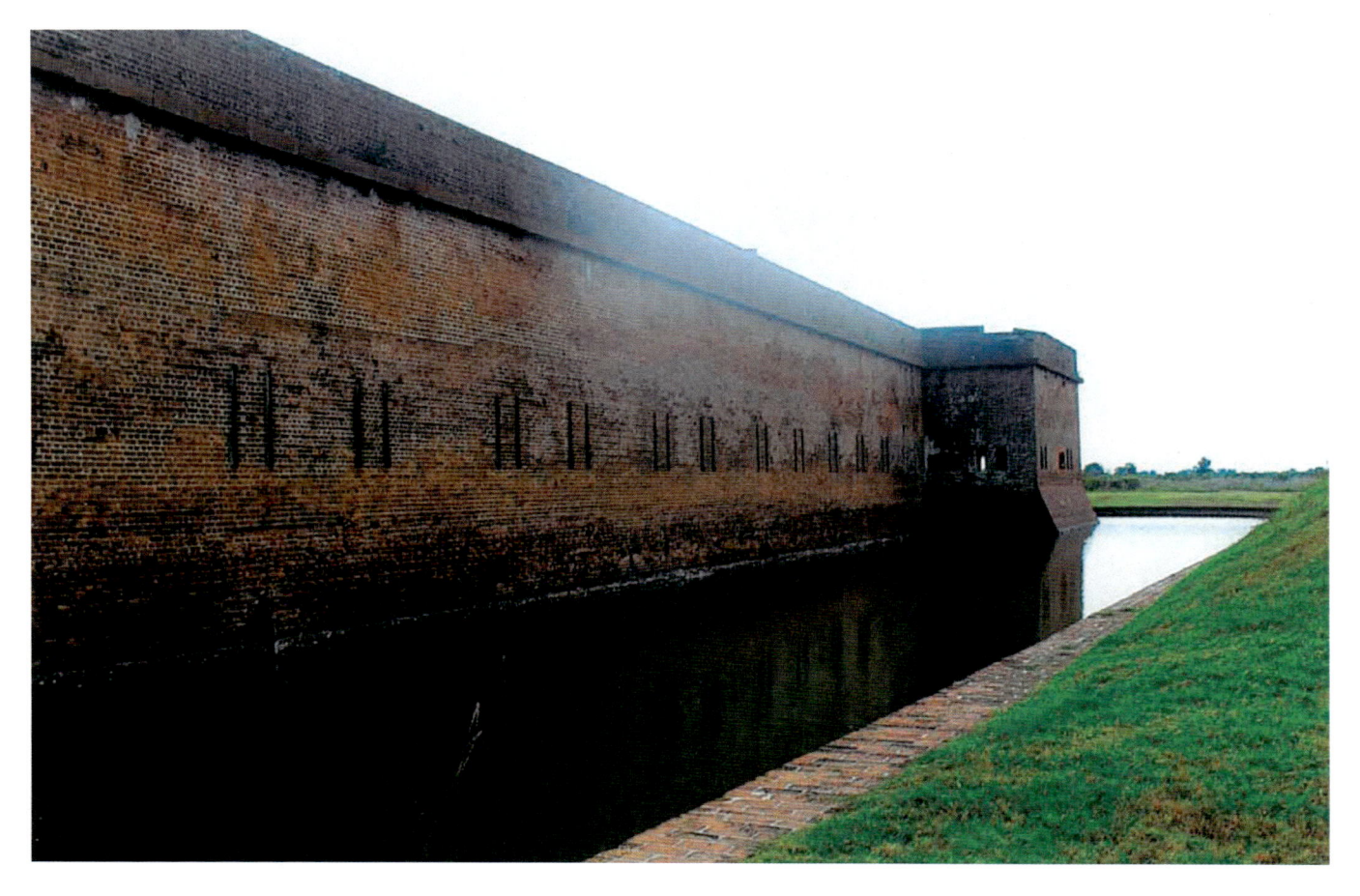

Pooler, GA. - Mighty Eighth Air Force Museum - 175 Bourne Av.

The Eighth Air Force was activated in 1942. Beautiful display of aviation and aviation art. Hall of Valor honors outstanding airmen who served with the Eighth.

Kennesaw, GA. - The General Locomotive - 2829 Cherokee St. NW

Great Locomotive Chase happened in April 1862. James Andrews, a union spy, stole the General. Andrews was captured an executed.

Warm Springs, GA. - Little White House - 401 Little White House Rd.

Personal retreat of Franklin D. Roosevelt, the 32nd President of the United States. He died here April 12, 1945

Andersonville, GA. - National historic site - 760 POW Rd.

Andersonville Prison, a Confederate POW Camp. Prison was commanded by Captain Henry Wirz who was execute after the war for war crimes. Approximately 1/3 of prisoners died

Ft. Stewart, GA. - Third Infantry Division Museum

158 Cavalry Way Building 506. This museum has on display Audie Murphy's M1 Carbine. Most decorated soldier of WWII.

Savannah, GA.

On December 22, 1864, General Sherman presented Savannah to President Lincoln as a Christmas gift. Sherman said, "Town was too pretty to burn." These cannons were captured when Lord Cornwallis surrendered at Yorktown in the American Revolution. During the Civil War these cannons were buried beneath the Chatham Armory, and were not removed until 1872 when the federals had departed.

Chickamauga - Battle of Chickamauga - TN. & GA. Line

Fought Sept. 18-20, 1863. First major battle fought in Georgia. Huge Union defeat in the Western Theater

Fitzgerald - Jefferson Davis Capture Site - 338 Jeff Davis Park Rd.

Visit the site where on May 10, 1865, Union Troops captured

Confederate President Jefferson Davis.

HAWAII

Pearl Harbor - Arizona, Oklahoma, Utah, Memorial

Dec. 7, 1941, America enters the Second World War. Arizona still burps oil today. Bullet holes can be seen in the hangars. Battleship Missouri, where Japanese surrendered, is docked here.

IDAHO

Montpelier, ID. - Butch Cassidy Museum - 833 Washington St.

Bank of Montpelier is the only bank in the country, robbed by Cassidy, still standing. Robbed bank August 13, 1896.

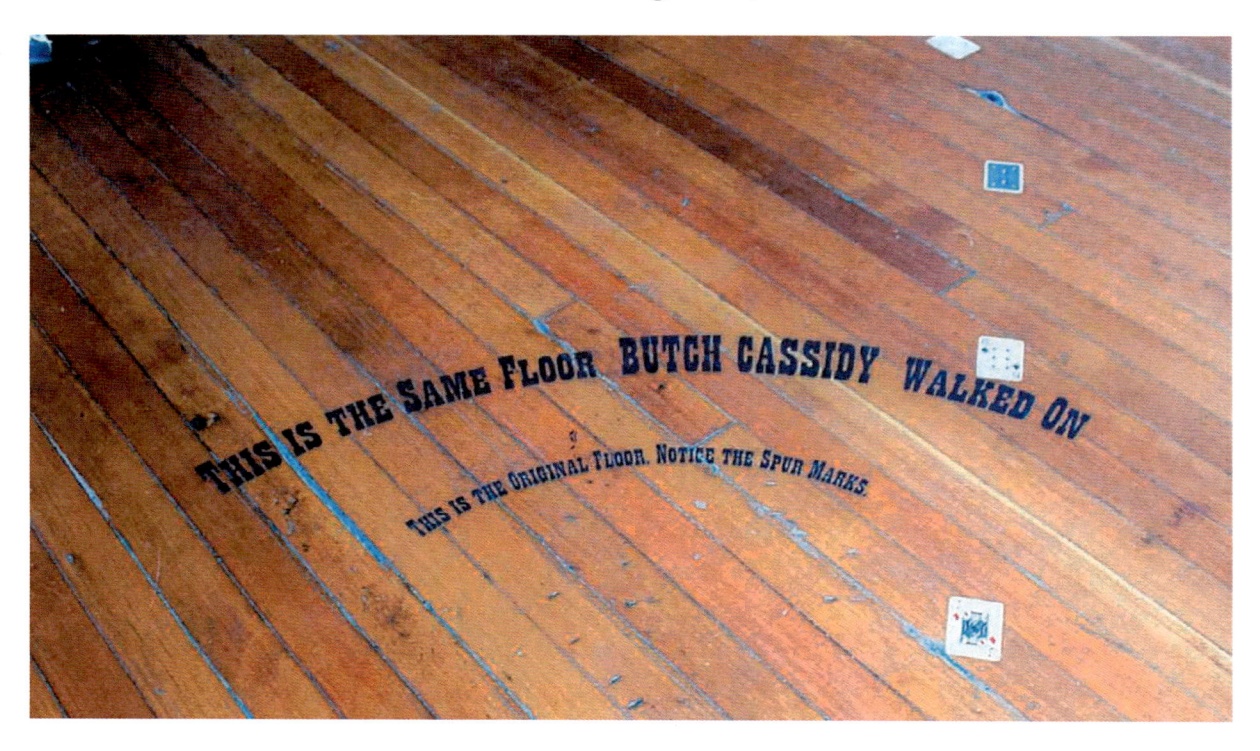

Oregon Trail - Passed through Idaho, and all along the trail you will see postings. Some spots you can still see remains of the trail. Lewis and Clark passed this way guided by Nez Perce Indians.

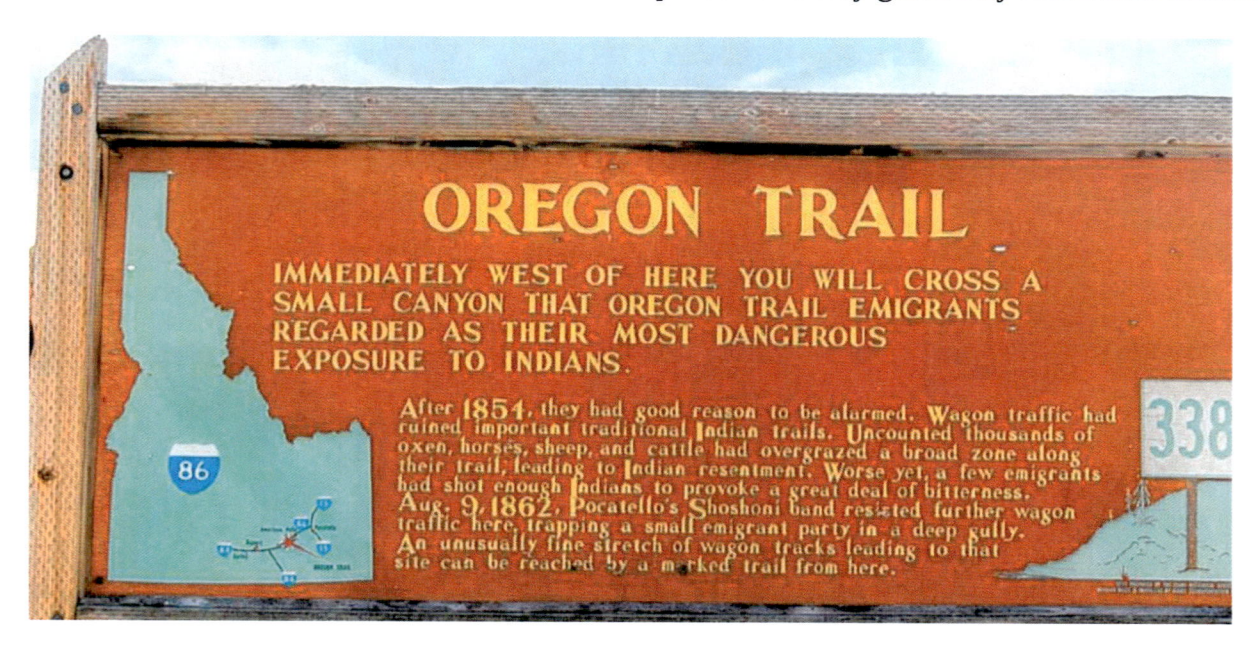

ILLINOIS

Dixon, IL. - Ronald Reagan Home - 816 S. Hennepin Av.

Home where 40th President of the United States lived as a young boy.

Tampico, IL. - Birthplace of Ronald Reagan - Main St.

Feb. 6, 1911, Ronald Wilson Reagan was born in an upstairs apartment. Tampico is also the birthplace of Admiral Joseph M. "Bull" Reeves, known as the "Father of Carrier Aviation."

Dixon, IL. John Deere Historic Site - 8334 S. Clinton St.

Home of John Deere. In 1837 in a small shop, he built the first steel plow.

In 1847 he moved to Moline, where he formed Deere & Company.

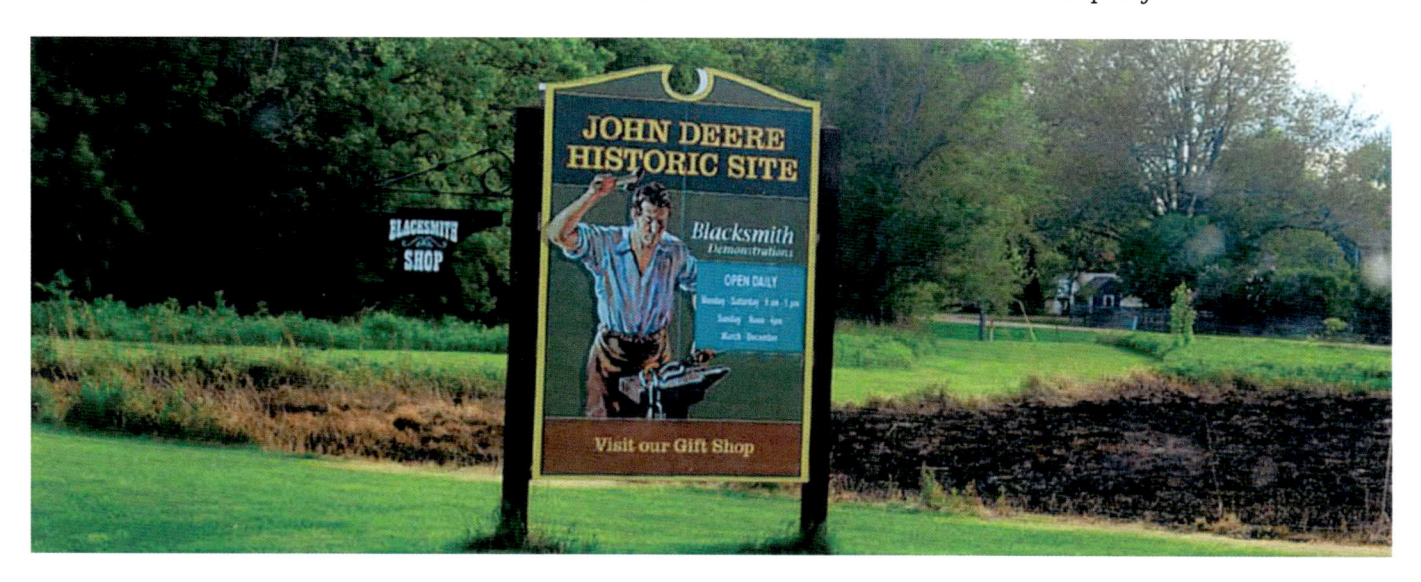

Troy Grove, IL. Wild Bill Hickok Memorial - 207 Peru St.

James Butler Hickok was born May 27, 1837

Served his country as a scout and spy in the western states for the Union during the Civil War. Was shot and killed in Deadwood, SD. August 2, 1876.

Monmouth, IL. - Wyatt Earp Birthplace - 406 S. 3rd St.

Earp was born here March 19, 1848. His full name was Wyatt Berry Stapp Earp.

Galena, IL. - Ulysses S. Grant Home - 511 Bouthillier St.

The home was a gift from the people of Galena in 1865 for his service to the country.

Springfield, IL. - Lincoln Home Historic Site - 413 S. 8th St.

Lincoln lived here 1844 to 1861 before becoming 16th President. He is buried in Oak Ridge Cemetery, 1500 Monument Av.

INDIANA

Lincoln City, IN. - Lincoln Boyhood Memorial - 3027 E S St.

Lincoln lived here from 1816 to 1830.

His mother Nancy Hanks Lincoln is buried here.

Hagerstown, IN. - Wilbur Wright Birthplace - 1525 N. County Rd. 750E

Wilbur Wright born here April 16, 1867.

With his brother Orville they began studying flight in 1896. They began gliding in 1900 and their first powered flight was in Kitty Hawk, NC Dec. 17, 1903

Crawfordsville, IN. - Gen. Lew Wallace Study - 200 Wallace Av.

Served in Union Army at Ft. Donelson, Shiloh, and managed operations when Morgan's Raiders invaded Indiana.

He served on Military Commission that tried John Wilkes Booth's assistants in the killing of President Lincoln. He also presided over the court that tried Henry Wirz who was Commander of Andersonville Prison. Most noted for his writing of Ben-Hur in 1880.

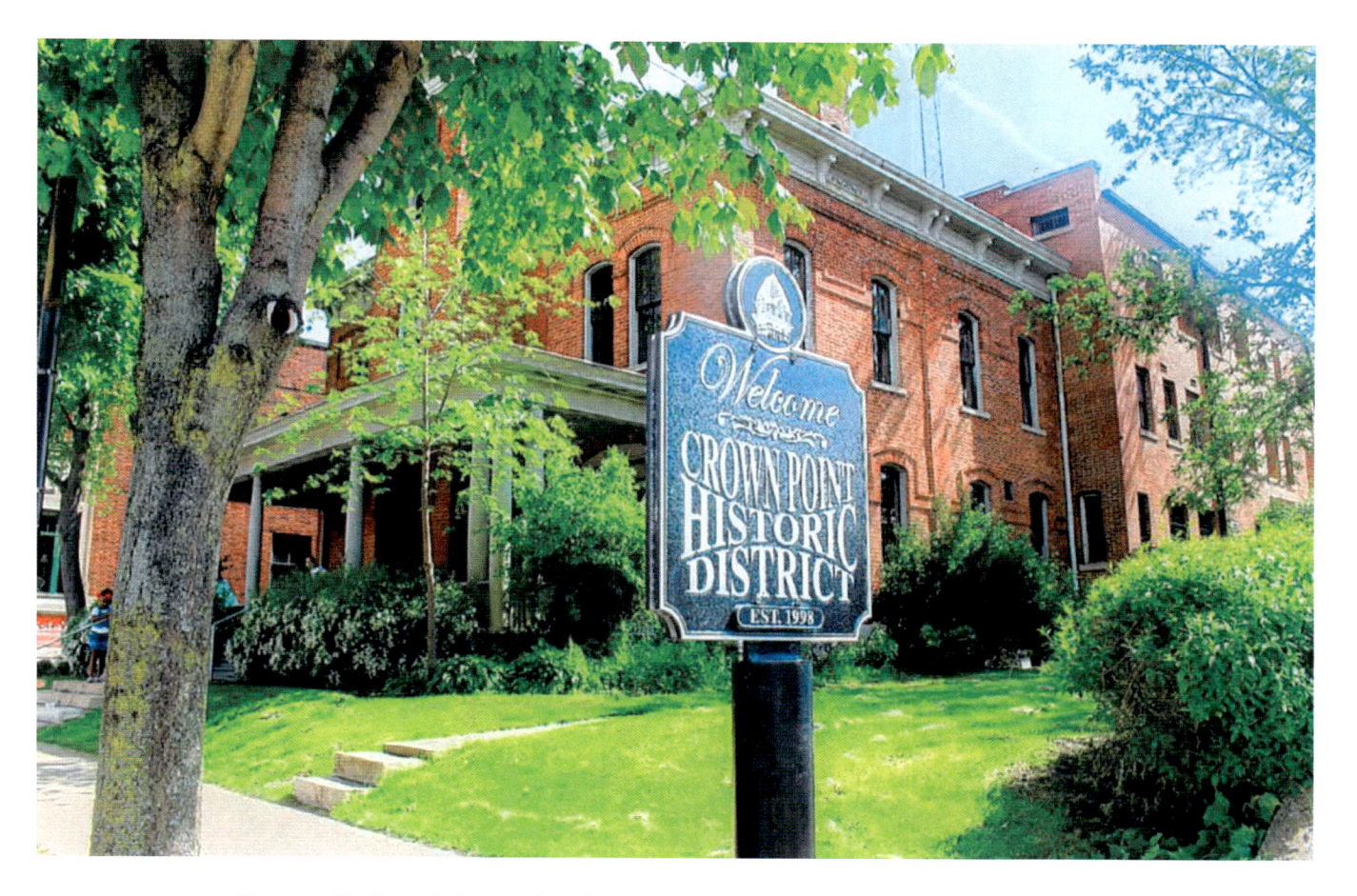

Crown Point, IN. - Lake County House & Jail - 232 S. Main St.

This jail was thought to be escape proof, till March 3, 1934, when John Dillinger proved them wrong. You can see his cell. He stole the sheriff's car to make his escape. On July 22nd of the same year, he was shot and killed by FBI outside of Biograph Theatre in Chicago. He is buried at Crown Hill Cemetery in Indianapolis.

Corydon, IN. - Battle of Corydon, July 9, 1863

General John Morgan and his 2,400 Cavalry invaded the north. It was the only battle in Indiana.

Lafayette, IN. - Battle of Tippecanoe - Nov. 7, 1811

General William Harrison engaged in battle with Indians of the Wabash Country led by the Prophet, brother of Indian leader Tecumseh. One day later Harrison and his troops burned and destroyed Prophetstown. Harrison became our ninth president.

IOWA

Adair, IA. - Jesse James Train Robbery - 1156 Anita - Adair Rd.

Site of the first train robbery in the west, by the James Gang. Actual section of track that was removed to wreck train. July 21, 1873

Ft. Madison, IA. - Ft. built in 1808

Black Hawks first battle against troops. Conditions here were so bad, that troops could not leave the fort. They couldn't even collect firewood. So, in 1813 they burned the fort and left.

Sioux City, IA. - Sergeant Floyd Monument - S. Lewis Blvd.

Charles Floyd was an explorer and quartermaster in Lewis & Clark Expedition. He became ill and died Aug. 20, 1804

Clear Lake, IA. - Buddy Holly Crash Site. - Feb. 3, 1959

Rockers Buddy Holly, Ritchie Valens, and "The Big Bopper" J.P. Richardson were killed in plane crash. "The day the music died" The site is marked by huge black glasses. Park and walk about ¼ mile through cornfield to crash site.

KANSAS

Abilene, KS. - Eisenhower Home - 201 SE 4th St.

Dwight Eisenhower lived here with his five brothers from 1898 to 1911 when he left for West Point at age 20.

Osawatomie, KS. - John Brown Museum - 1000 Main St.

Contains the cabin John Brown lived in for 20 months conducting his abolitionist activities.

Lawrence, KS. - Comanche Horse - 1450 Jayhawk Blvd.

University of Kansas Natural History Museum you can see the horse that survived the battle of the Little Bighorn

Hays, KS - Ft. Hays

Active from 1865 till 1889 was frontier post during Indian Wars.

Marysville, KS. - Pony Express Home Station - 106 S. 8th St.

This barn was a Pony Express Station April 1860 till October 1861. One stop on a 1966-mile journey.

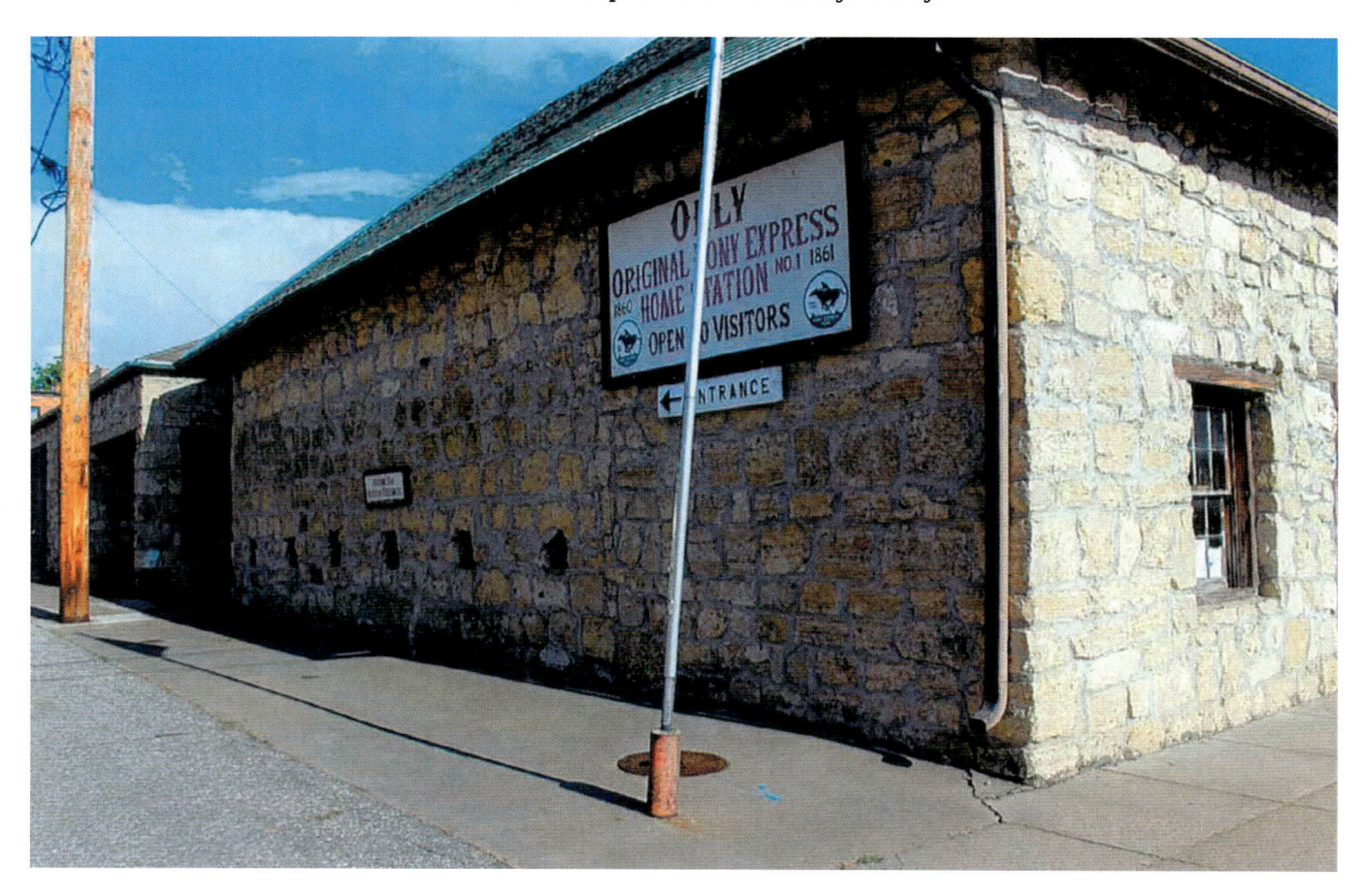

Hanover, KS. - Hollenberg Pony Express Station. Built in 1858

It is the most intact surviving station of the Pony Express located at 2889 23rd. Rd.

Dodge City, KS.

Named for nearby Fort Dodge. Wild frontier town of the old west. Walk the streets of deputies Wyatt Earp, Bat Masterson and Gambler Doc Holiday. Tour the Long Branch Saloon.

KENTUCKY

Ft. Knox - United States Bullion Depository - Gold Vault Rd.

Constructed in 1936. First gold brought here by railroad in 1937. No public visits or tours.

Fairview, KY - Jefferson Davis Birthplace - 351 Foot Obelisk.

The only president of the Confederate States of America was born here June 3, 1808

Bowling Green, KY - Lost River Cave - 2818 Nashville Rd.

During Civil War the cave was under control by north & south at different times. John Hunt Morgan hid in cave from Union Soldiers. Jesse James also used cave.

Williamson, KY. - Noah's Ark - 1 Ark Encounter Dr.

Large ship built to Biblical Measurements

Tug Fork of the Big Sandy River - Hatfield and McCoy Feud

From 1863-1891. Randall McCoy's Well, the Hog Trial Cabin, Devil Anse Hatfield grave are just some of sites available to view.

Hodgenville, KY - Abraham Lincoln Birthplace - 2995 Lincoln Farm Rd.

Place where Lincoln was born and lived his early childhood

Boonesborough, KY. - Founded by Frontiersman Daniel Boone

In 1778 as one of first English Settlements west of the Appalachian Mountains.

Ft. Knox, KY - Gen. George Patton Museum - 4554 Fayette Av.

Dedicated to the memory of George Patton

LOUISIANA

New Orleans - National WWII Museum - 945 Magazine St.

Excellent Museum telling the story of the war that changed the world.

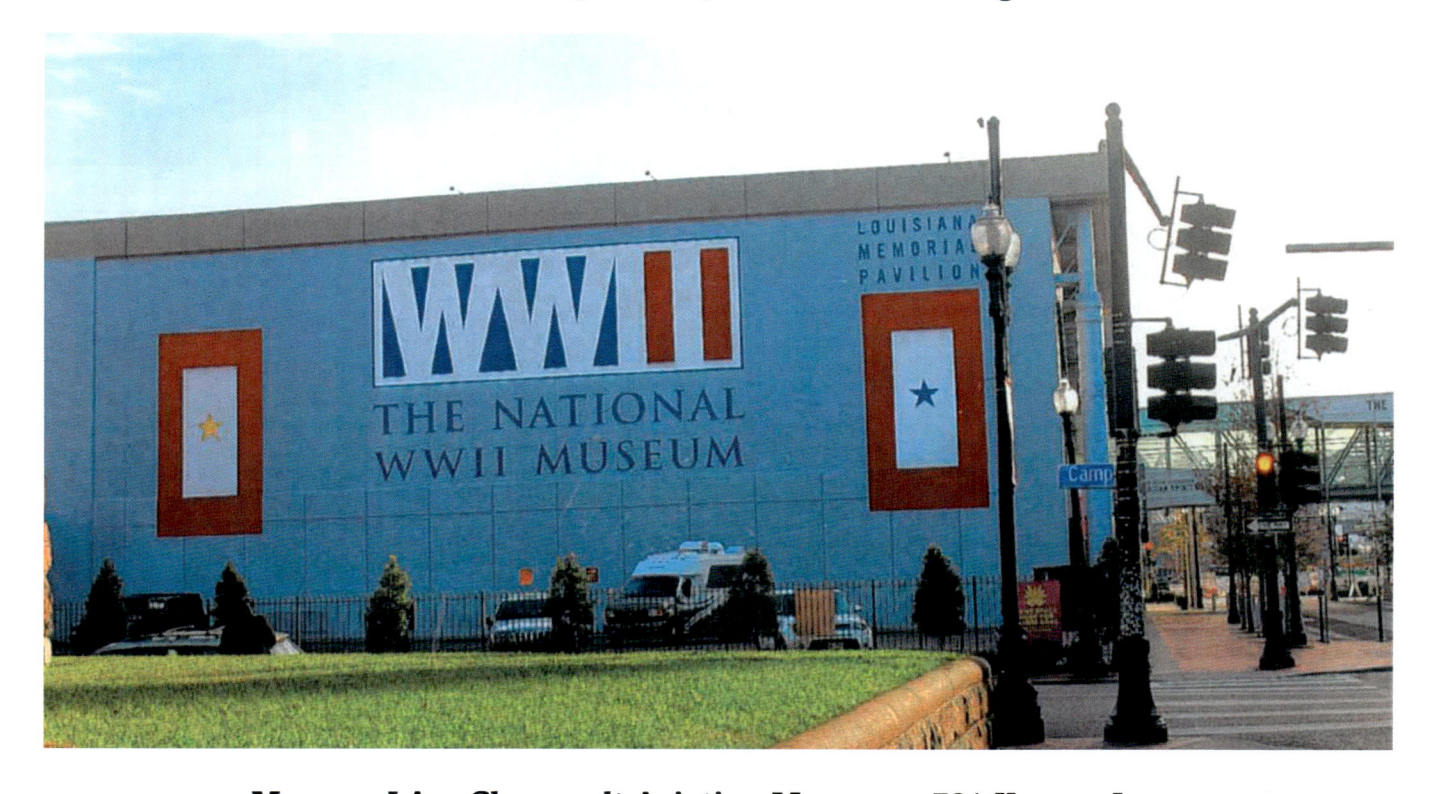

Monroe, LA. - Chennault Aviation Museum - 701 Kansas Lane

Honoring Veterans from WWI through Iraqi freedom. Also honors Gen. Chennault and the Flying Tigers.

Gibsland, LA. - Bonnie & Clyde Ambush Museum - 2419 Main St.

Their reign of terror ran from 1930 through 1934. Believed to have murdered 9 police officers, and 4 civilians. Killed May 1934 by ambush outside of Gibsland.

Stone monument marks the ambush.

New Orleans - Jackson Square - 701 Decatur St.

A must see in the French quarter. Plans for battle of New Orleans were at Pierre Maspero's exchange corner of Charles & St. Louis Av.

Vacherie, LA. - Oak Alley Plantation

Built 1837-39 famous for its evenly spaced 28 live oak trees.

Chalmette, LA. - Battlefield - 1 Battlefield Rd.

Site of last major battle of the war of 1812. Fought on Jan. 8, 1815. Led by General Andrew Jackson they defeated a much large force of British soldiers.

Baton Rouge - USS Kidd DD-661 305 S. River Rd.

Named after Rear Admiral Isaac C. Kidd who died on the bridge of his flagship USS Arizona. The only surviving US destroyer still in her World War II condition.

MARYLAND

Baltimore - Fort McHenry - 2400 E. Fort Av.

War of 1812 when the Fort defended Baltimore Harbor. Inspired Francis Scott key to write "The Star-Spangled Banner".

Annapolis - Crypt of John Paul Jones - 121 Blake Rd.

Referred as the "The Father of the American Navy" Best Naval Commander of his time.

Mount Savage - Mt. Savage Iron Works

Operated 1837 to 1868. First to produce iron rails for railroad.

Cumberland - George Washington's Headquarters - 38 Greene St.

Commanded Virginia Troops during French and Indian War.

Sharpsburg - Antietam Battlefield - 302 E. Main St.

Gen. Lee's first invasion of the north. Sept. 17, 1862. Bloodiest day in United States history. Over 22,000 dead, wounded or missing.

Clinton - Surratt House - 9110 Brandywine Rd.

Built in 1852. John Wilkes Booth was to stop here as he fled after killing Pres. Lincoln. The rifle he was to receive is on the wall here.

Waldorf - Dr. Samuel Mudds Home - 3725 Samuel Mudd Rd.

April 15th, 1865, Dr Mudd splinted Booth's leg.

Grantsville - Castlemans River Bridge - 10240 National Pike

Built 1813. Largest stone arch bridge in America at the time. Continuously used till 1933.

Samples Manor - John Brown Raid Headquarters

John Brown and his associates collected arms & ammunition on the Kennedy Farm prior to raid on arsenal at Harpers Ferry

Baltimore - USS Constellation - 301 E. Pratt St.

Built 1853-1855, the last sail-only warship built by the United States Navy. During the Civil War she served in the Mediterranean looking for Confederate ships. Original constellation built in 1797 broke up in 1853.

MASSACHUSETTS

Concord - North Bridge - "Shot Heard Round the World"

April 19, 1775, fighting lasted only a few seconds. Marked the beginning of the war for independence.

Boston - Bunker Hill Monument - Monument Square

Site of battle between British and Patriots. June 17, 1775, Take the Freedom Trail around Boston to see it all.

Boston - Old State House - 206 Washington St.

Built in 1713, Seat of General Court till 1798. One of the oldest public buildings in the United States.

Boston - Old North Church - 193 Salem St.

Famous for "One If By Land, Two If By Sea" related to Paul Revere's ride of April 18, 1775

Boston - Paul Revere House - 19 North Square

Built in 1680. Home to Paul Revere during the American Revolution. It's the oldest house in Boston

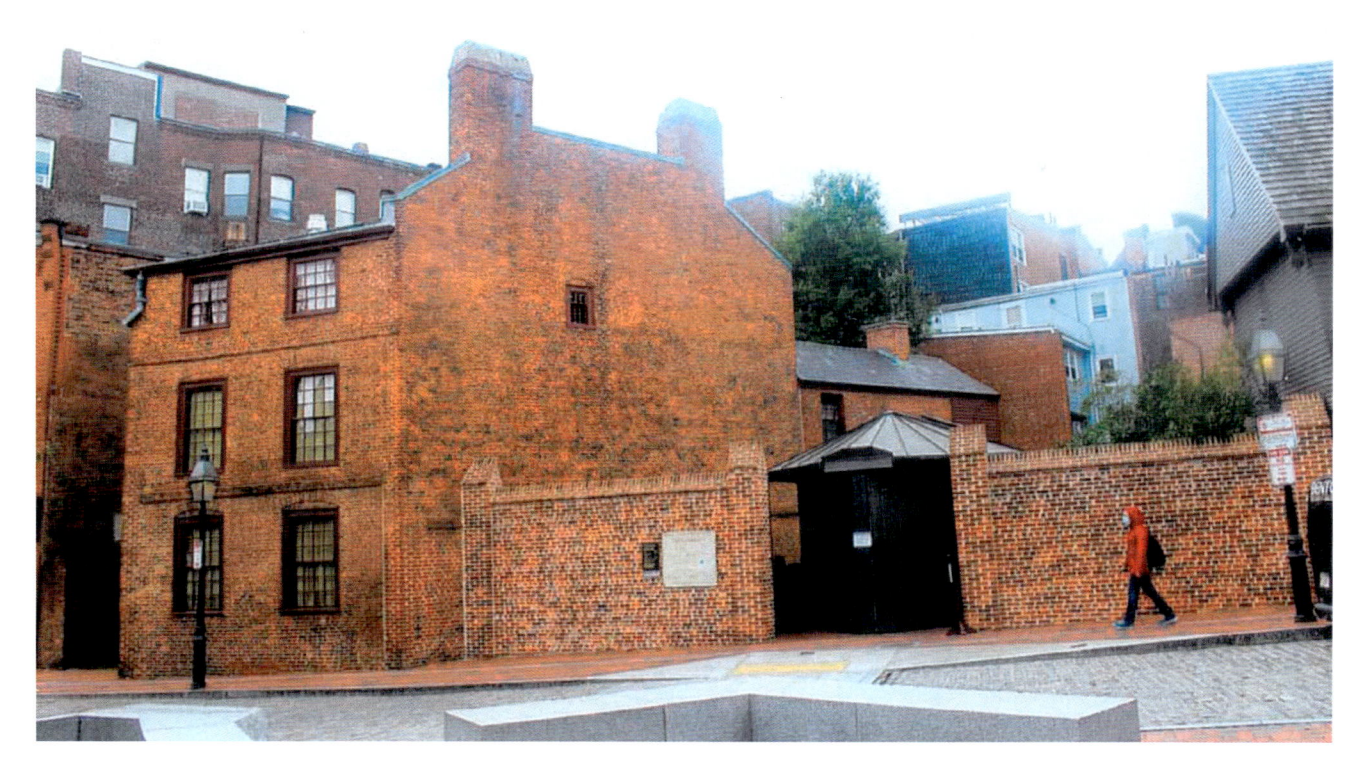

Boston - Granary Burying Ground - Tremont St.

Final resting place for many revolutionary patriots Paul Revere, three signers of Declaration of Independence Samuel Adams, Robert Paine, John Hancock. Five victims of Boston Massacre are also buried here.

Boston - JFK Presidential Library Columbia Point

Library to the 35th President. See the coconut that Kennedy carved a message on to have the crew of PT 109 rescued.

Boston - Tea Party 306 Congress St.

On Dec. 16, 1773, Sons of Liberty protested the taxes. The protesters, some disguised as Indians, destroyed a shipment of tea. See replica of the ship.

Concord - Barrett's Farm 448 Barrett's Mill Rd.

Farm was storage for militia gunpowder, weapons and 2 pair of bronze cannons.

MICHIGAN

Monroe - Gen. Custer Monument - Elm Av.
He lived here much of his early childhood.

Monroe - River Raisin Battlefield - 333 N. Dixie Hwy
During war 1812, was the Battle of Frenchtown. Jan. 18-23, 1813.
397 Americans were killed and 547 taken prisoners.

Mackinaw City - Mackinaw Point Lighthouse
Operational from 1890 to 1957. Marks the junction of Lake Michigan and Lake Huron.
One of the busiest crossroads of the Great Lakes. Light was visible for 16 miles.

Dearborn - Henry Ford Museum - 20900 Oakwood Blvd.
Museum is loaded with artifacts - Pres. Kennedy's limo, Lincolns chair from Ford's Theatre, Thomas Edison's laboratory, Rosa Parks bus, and Wright Brothers bicycle shop.

MINNESOTA

Mankato - Dakota War of 1862

Site of the largest one-day mass execution in American history.

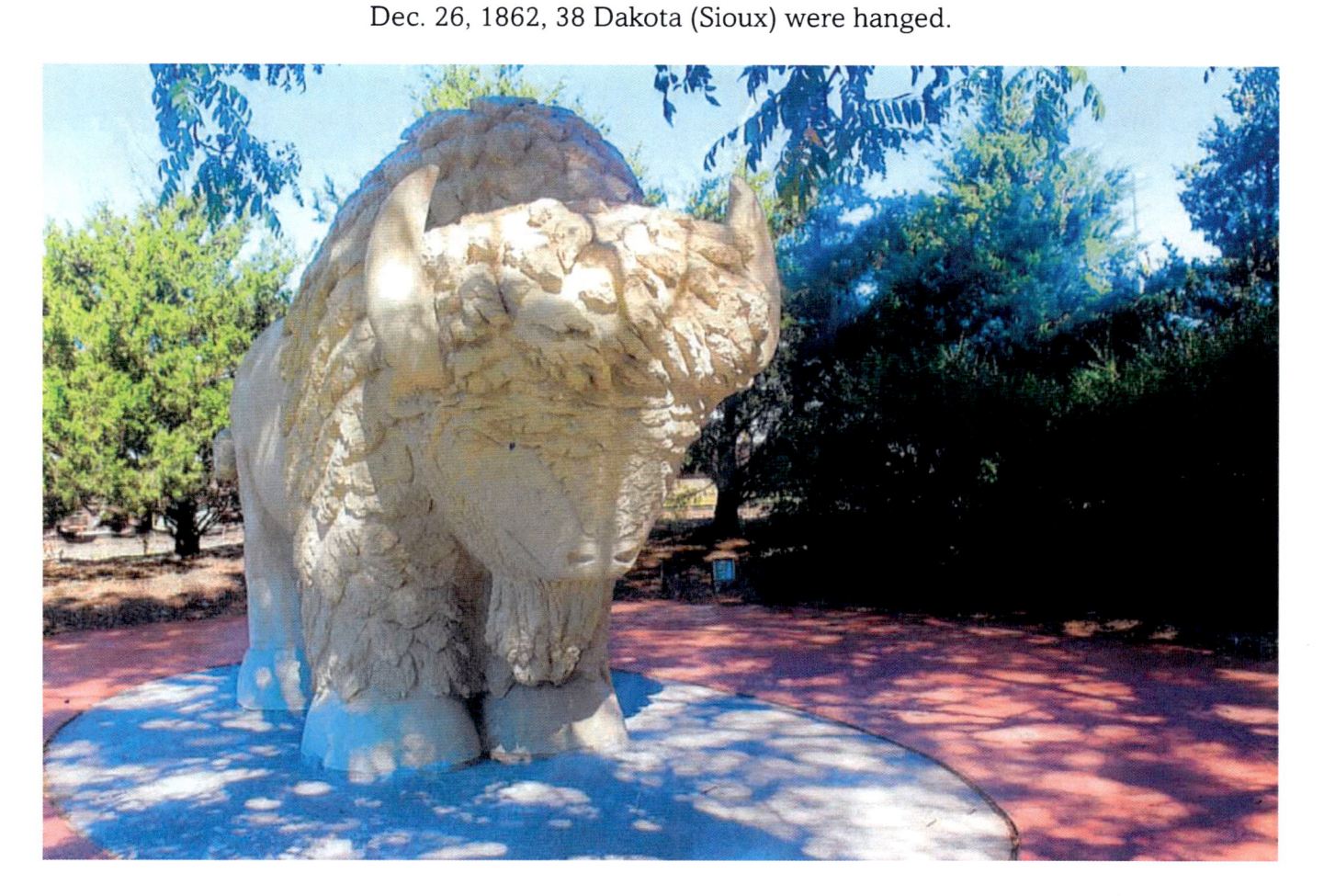

Dec. 26, 1862, 38 Dakota (Sioux) were hanged.

Beaver Bay Township - Split Rock Lighthouse State Park

One of the most picturesque lighthouses in America. Built in 1940 in response to 29 ships being lost.

Walnut Grove - Laura Ingalls Museum - 330 8th St.

Writer known for Little House on the Prairie Series.

MISSISSIPPI

Biloxi - Beauvoir - 2244 Beach Blvd.
Was post war home of Jefferson Davis. 1876-1889

Vicksburg - National Battlefield
Site of 47-day siege of the city to starve them out

Gen. Pemberton surrendered on July 4, 1863, one day after Lee's defeat at Gettysburg.

Marked turning point of Civil War.

Vicksburg - USS Cairo
USS Cairo struck a mine Dec. 12, 1862, an sunk in 12 minutes to the bottom of the Mississippi. Was found in 1956. Can be seen at Vicksburg Museum.

Rolling Fork - Onward Store - 6693 Hwy 61

Nov. 4, 1902, Pres. Theodore Roosevelt while on a hunting trip refused to shoot a captive bear. This led to the creation of the Teddy Bear.

Port Gibson - Civil War Battle

Confederate Forces clashed with Union Forces commanded by Gen.

Grant. Grant said, Port Gibson was to pretty to burn. Nearby is Rodney Presbyterian Church which survived the battle. Cannon ball remains inside of church building.

Glen Allan - St. John's Church - 286 Eastside Lake Washington Rd.

Window lead used for bullets during Civil War.

Port Gibson - Windsor Ruins - 10 miles SW of Port Gibson

Mansion stood from 1861 to 1890. It was destroyed by fire.

Ellisville - Amos Deason Home - 410 Anderson St.

Oct. 5, 1863, Confederate Major Amos McLemore, who was rounding up deserters, was shot and killed by Newton Knight. "Free State of Jones" movie is about this.

Natchez - Natchez Trace Trail

Trail covers 440 miles from Natchez, MS to Nashville, TN. Trail has many landmarks along the way. Beautiful ride.

Tupelo - Elvis Presley Birthplace - 306 Elvis Presley Dr.

Birthplace home of Elvis Presley. Born Jan. 3, 1935

MISSOURI

Defiance - Daniel Boone Home - 1868 Hwy F

House was built by Nathan Boone his son.

Home was completed in 1810. The walls are 2½ ft. thick.

Daniel Boone died here Sept. 26, 1820, at age 86.

He's buried nearby.

Laclede - Gen. John Pershing Boyhood Home

Leader of American Expeditionary Forces in World War I. Lived in this home from age six to adulthood.

St. Louis - Grant's Farm - 10501 Gravois Rd.

Built by Ulysses S. Grant on land given to him by his father. Check out the Clydesdales on the farm, plus other wild animals.

Independence - Harry Truman Library - 500 W. US Hwy 24 "The Buck Stops Here"

St. Joseph - Patee House - 12th & Penn St.

Pony Express Headquarters 1861. 1996 miles in 10 days.

140 room luxury hotel.

St. Joseph - Jesse James Home - 1201 S. 12th St.

James was murdered in this house April 3, 1882

Liberty - Jesse James Bank Museum - 103 N. Water St.

Site of nations first daylight bank robbery.

You will see the bank as it was in 1866, day of the robbery.

Kearney - James Grave Site - Mt. Olivet Cemetery - E. 6th St.

Sibley - Fort Osage

Built in 1808 as a trading post, and to protect the Osage from tribal enemies. William Clark was appointed Indian agent for the territory.

Hannibal - Mark Twain Boyhood Home - 120 N. Main St.

Home of Samuel Langhorne Clemens, better known as Mark Twain from 1844 to 1853.

Hannibal - Molly Brown - 600 Butler St.

Birthplace of Titanic's unsinkable Molly Brown Born 1867, Margaret Tobin Brown, hero of the Titanic. Learn of her rags-to-riches life.

MONTANA

Little Bighorn River - Battle of the Little Bighorn
Custer's last stand - June 25-26, 1876

Ft. Benton - 2nd Oldest Settlement in Montana 1846
Founded as a fur post. Trails led to all points carrying supplies to the

U.S. and Canada steamboats docked at Ft. Benton's Levee. Nearby is Montana Memorial to Lewis & Clark. 1722 Front St.

Browning - Camp Disappointment - 12 miles East of Browning
North side of Rt. 2. Marks the farthest point north reached by Lewis & Clark.

Nevada City and Virginia City - Gold camps along Alder Gulch 1863.
They were the largest. Known as one of the richest gold strikes in the Rocky Mountain West.

Pompey's Pillar - Signature of William Clark - 3039 Hwy 312

William Clark signed this rock on July 25, 1806

Physical evidence that you are standing in the footsteps of William Clark.

Butte - Dumas Brothel - 45 E. Mercury St.

Brothel was founded in 1890 by two French Canadian brothers Joseph and Arthur Nadeau. Closed in 1982, as the longest operating brothel in the United States.

NEBRASKA

Bayard - Chimney Rock Museum - 9822 County Rd. 75

Chimney rock rises 300 feet and served as landmark along the Oregon Trail. Nearby was Chimney Rock Station a stop for the Pony Express.

Gothenburg - Pony Express Station - 510 15th St.

Used as Pony Express Stop from 1860 to 1861. Erected in 1854 on the Oregon Trail as a ranch house and trading post.

Kearney - Fort Kearny Historical Park - 1020 V Rd.

Founded in 1848 along the Oregon Trail. Wagons could resupply here on their journey west. Safe rest stop going west.

Omaha - Gen. Crook's House - 5730 N. 30th St.

Built in 1879. Gen. Crook was the only commander to occupy the house. Gen. Crook invited Mr. & Mrs. Grant to visit in 1879.

NEVADA

Virginia City - Boomtown 1859

1859 discovery of the Comstock Lode, major silver discovery in the United States.

Middlegate - Middlegate Station - Rt. 50

Located along "The Loneliest Road in America" Rt. 50

A must stop if you like a good hamburger.

Austin - Cold Springs Station Site - 51 miles West of Austin Rt. 50

1861-1869 was a passenger and freight station. Stone ruins remain. Nearby is location of Pony Express Station.

Winnemucca - Martin Hotel - 94 W. Railroad St.

Built in 1913. Served as boarding house for sheepherders.

Mercury - Constructed for Atomic Energy Commission.

It's a closed village started in 1950. Flourished till 1992, when subcritical nuclear testing stopped.

NEW JERSEY

Morristown - Ford Mansion - 30 Washington Place

Built in 1774 and was headquarters for George Washington from Dec. 1779 to June 1780 during Revolutionary War.

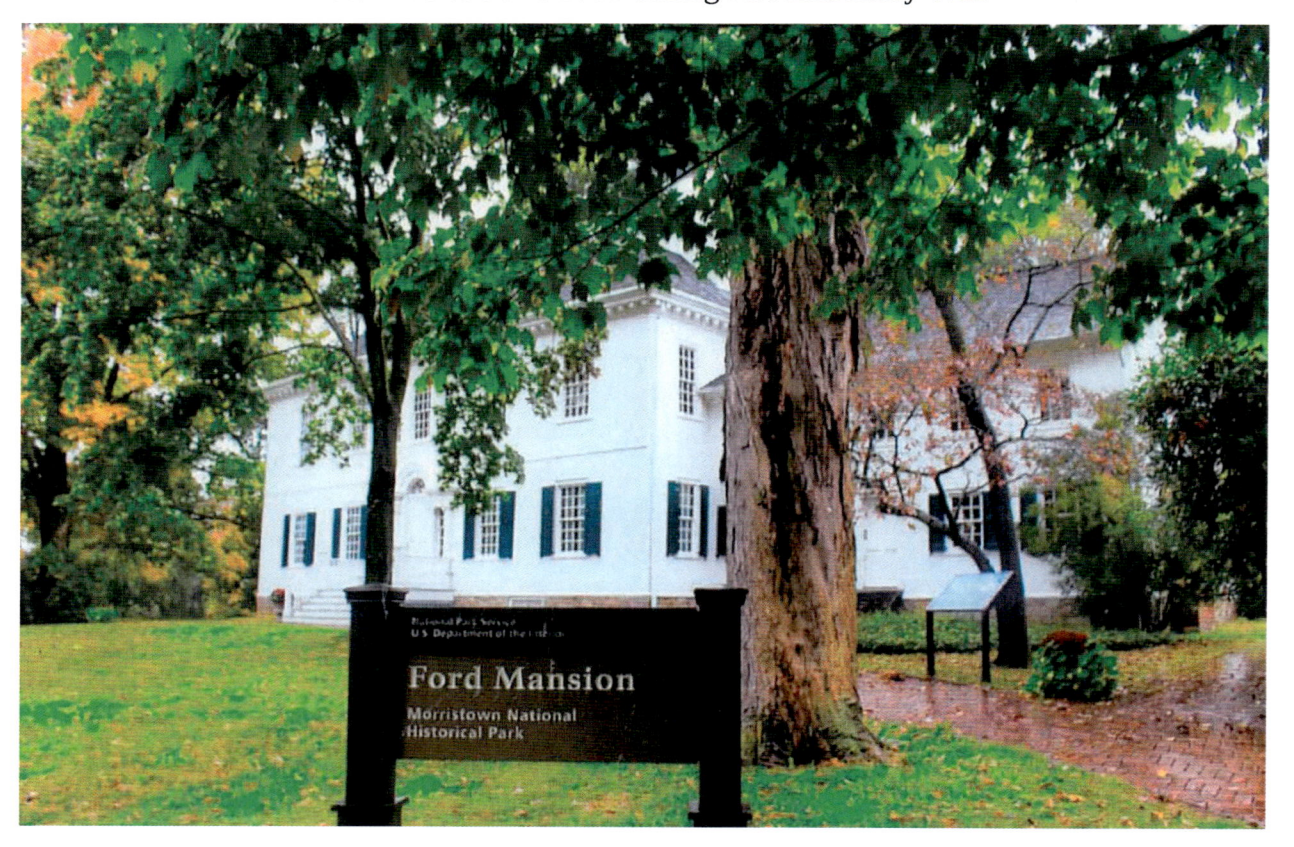

Princeton - Battlefield Monument. - 55 Stockton St.

Commemorates the Jan. 3, 1777, Battle of Princeton and shows George Washington leading his troops to victory.

Morristown - Fort Nonsense - 30 Washington Place

Occupies a hilltop overlooking Morristown. Built by Continental Army in the Winter of 1779-80

Trenton - Battle Monument

Commemorates Dec. 26, 1776, Battle for Trenton, a victory for the Continental Army.

Jersey City - Ellis Island - Immigration Processing

First inspection station opened in 1892. Used as POW camp for both World Wars.

NEW MEXICO

Lincoln - Lincoln County Courthouse - U.S. 380

Billy the Kids famous escape April 1881 looks much like it did during Lincoln County War 1878-1881

Old Fort Sumner Cemetery - Billy the Kid's Grave

July 14, 1881, Pat Garrett shot and killed Billy the Kid

Capitan - Fort Stanton - 7 mi. SE of Capitan near U.S. 380

Built in 1855 as base against Mescalero Apaches was abandoned in 1896

Los Alamos Atomic City

Birthplace of the Atomic Age. Manhattan project during WWII

Las Cruces - Pat Garrett Murder Site - East on Hwy 70

Killed over land dispute with Jesse Brazel. Shot in the stomach and head.

NEW YORK

Ticonderoga - Ft. Ticonderoga - 102 Fort T. Rd.

Built 1755-1757 during "Seven Years War". Great men have passed through the gate to the Fort. George Washington, Benjamin Franklin, Benedict Arnold, Ethan Allen to name a few.

Mount Defiance - Near Ft. Ticonderoga

853 ft. high hill overlooking Lake Champlain and Ft. Ticonderoga. 1777 British occupied this hill causing the Americans to withdraw from Fort without a fight.

West Point - United States Military Academy

Established as a Fort overlooking the Hudson River.

Gen. George Custer is buried here. Oldest of the five service academies.

Rome - Fort Stanwix National Monument - 200 N. James St.

Built in 1758 by the British. Captured by the Americans, British Army besieged the Fort, but failed to retake it.

Stillwater - Saratoga Historical Park - 648 NY-32

Marks the first American victory of the Revolutionary War. After battle in 1777, France recognizes the Independence of the United States. Park contains Boot Monument to Benedict Arnold Monument also to Morgan's Light Corps and other American troops

Lake George - Fort William Henry

Built in 1755 during French and Indian War by the British. The French captured the Fort in 1757. The British surrendered, with the French Army killing most of the British prisoners.

New York- Liberty Park

Park at the Twin Towers 155 Cedar St. Manhattan

New York - Horse Soldiers Memorial 180 Greenwich St Manhattan

Dedicated to the first combat troops deployed to Afghanistan.

Long Island - Setauket - Revolutionary Spy Ring 93 N Country Rd.

Gen. George Washington Culper Spy Ring organized by Maj. Tallmadge. Leaders were Abraham Woodhull, Robert Townsend, and Anna

Strong. Several points of interest in Setauket and Oyster Bay.

NORTH CAROLINA

Kill Devil Hills - Wright Brothers Memorial - 1000 N. Croatan Hwy

Marks the birth of flight. Wilbur and Orville Wright came here from Dayton, Ohio based on information about steady wind. Orville was first to fly a distance of 120 ft. Dec. 17, 1903

Roanoke Island - Outer Banks

Birthplace of America's first English child 1587, Virginia Dare

Durham - Bennett Place - 4409 Bennett Memorial Rd.

Farmhouse of James Bennett where Gen. Joseph E. Johnston surrendered to Union Gen. William Sherman April 26, 1865

Kure Beach - Fort Fisher - 1610 Ft. Fisher Blvd

Confederate Fort during the Civil War protecting trade routes of the Port of Wilmington. It's fall Jan. 15, 1865, closed Wilmington, thus sealing the fate of the confederacy.

Four Oaks - Bentonville Battlefield Site - 5466 Harper House Rd.

Site of 1865 Battle of Bentonville, fought in the last days of Civil War. Gen. Sherman against Gen. Johnston was largest battle in North Carolina.

Fayetteville - Airborne & Special Operations Museum - 100 Bragg Blvd.

History of U.S. Army Airborne & Special Operations Forces. Contains wreckage of Super 6-1 Black Hawk shot down in Mogadishu. Exhibit to "Monuments Men" is also here.

Buxton - Cape Hatteras Lighthouse - Outer Banks

210 ft tall, first lit in 1803. Seen from 24 miles away

NORTH DAKOTA

Washburn - Fort Mandan - 12 miles from Washburn.

Built 1804 as winter encampment for Lewis & Clark. Lewis & Clark first met Sacagawea here. Her son was born here Feb. 11, 1805, which she took with her during the expedition.

Williston - Ft Union Trading Post

Built in 1828 and was run by John Jacob Astor's American Fur Company until 1867.

Busiest trading post on the upper Missouri.

Morton - Fort Abraham Lincoln - 7 miles South of Mandan

Built in 1872 - 1873 the 7th Cavalry arrived to ensure the expansion of the Northern Pacific Railway. General Custer's last home is here. In 1876 Custer and his men left as part of the Great Sioux War. Custer never returned.

OHIO

Dayton- Museum of the U.S. Air Force- 1100 Spaatz St.

Contains many rare aircraft. Memphis Belle and Bockscar, B-29 that dropped Fat Man bomb on Nagasaki.

Dayton - Wright Brothers Cycle Shop - 22 S. William St.

Business began in 1892. They used profits from Cycle shop to finance their aviation. Wheels to wings.

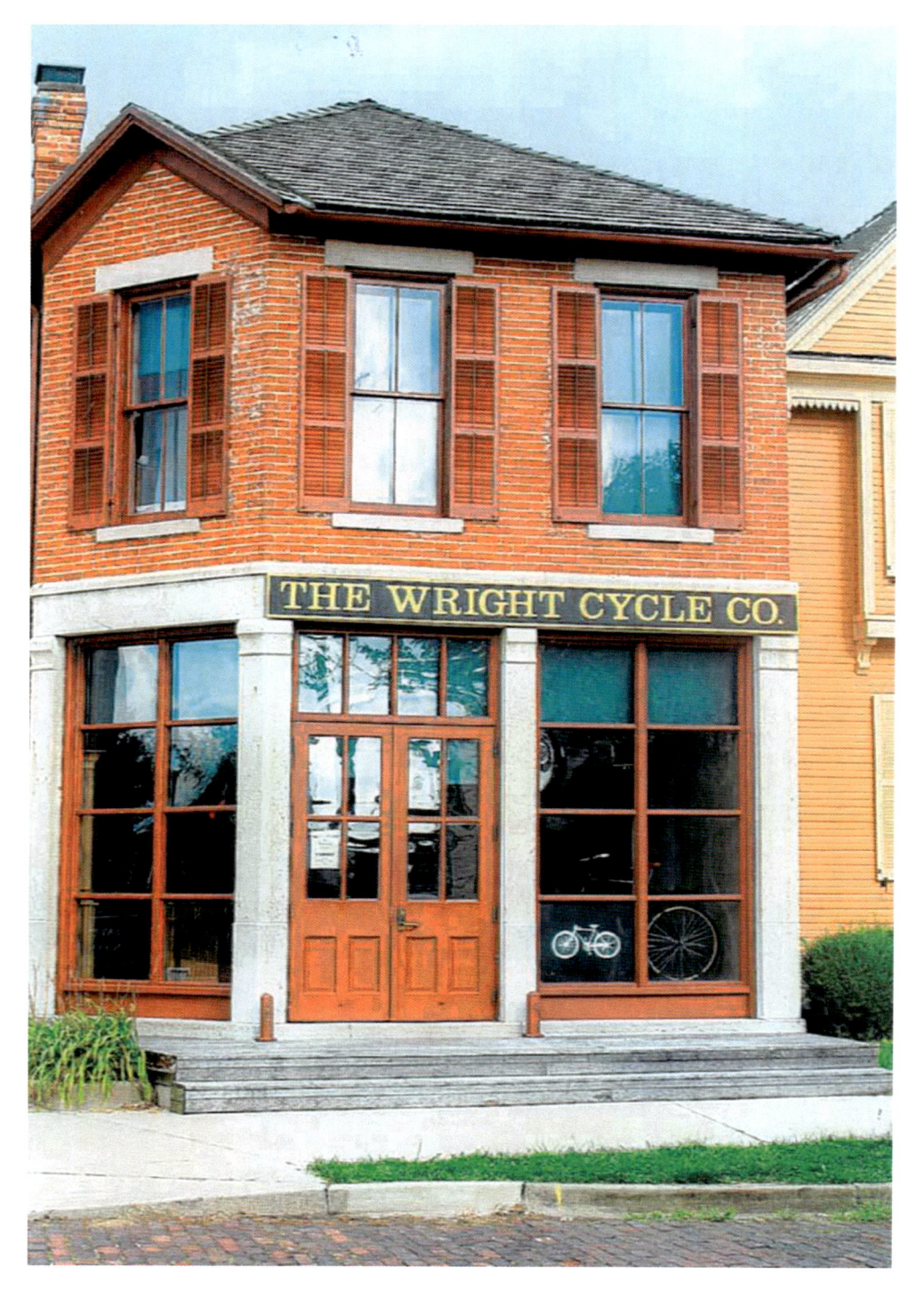

Wapakoneta - Armstrong Air & Space Museum - 500 Apollo Dr.

First man to set foot on the moon. Ohio's contribution to air and space, including Gemini 8 spacecraft piloted by Armstrong to perform first space docking

Georgetown - U.S. Grant Boyhood Home - 219 E. Grant Av.
Built in 1823 Grant lived in this house from 1824 to 1839.

Milan - Birthplace of Thomas Alva Edison - 9 Edison Dr.
One of America's important inventors was born 1847.

New Rumley - George Armstrong Custer Birthplace - Route 646
Custer Memorial is all that is here. He was born here Dec. 5, 1839. Died June 25, 1876, Battle of Little Big Horn.

Jackson - Morgan's Raiders
Morgan's raid can be followed from Cincinnati, across Southern Ohio (Rt. 32) to where he surrendered near West Point near Salineville, OH. Farthest north of any Confederate Army.

Lancaster - Sherman House Museum - 137 E. Main St.
Childhood home of Gen. William T. Sherman

OKLAHOMA

Oklahoma City - Alfred P. Murrah Building - 620 N. Harvey Av.

Bombing took place April 19, 1995. Domestic terrorist truck bombing by Timothy McVeigh and Terry Nichols. Killing 168 people and injured 680 others

Lawton - Fort Sill - 85 Miles Southwest of Oklahoma City

Built in 1869 and still in use today as Field Artillery School. Built for Indian Wars. Geronimo was held here as POW and is buried at Apache Indian Cemetery inside Fort Sill.

Bartlesville - Frank Phillips Home - 1107 S. Cherokee Av.

Founder of Phillips Petroleum in Bartlesville in 1917.

Tulsa - Golden Driller - Titanic Oil Man - 4145 E. 21st

Tallest free - standing statue in the United States. 76 feet.

Ft. Gibson - Oldest Town in Oklahoma - Cherokee County

Established in 1824, was abandoned in 1890 Cherokee's

Trail of Tears ended nearby at Tahlequah.

Oklahoma City - Centennia Land Run Monument - 200 Centennial Av.

Commemorates the Land Run of 1889, 50,000 Americans vying for land. A great monument for these Americans.

Bartlesville - Nellie Johnstone No. 1 - Johnstone Park

First commercially productive oil well in Oklahoma completed in April 1897 and abandoned in 1964.

Ingalls - Battle of Ingalls

Sept. 1, 1893, Ingalls was a gunfight between U.S. Marshalls and the Doolin- Dalton Gang. Doolin-Dalton Gang fled Ingalls 3 marshals were killed.

OREGON

Astoria - Fort Clatsop - 92345 Ft. Clatsop Rd.

In 1802 Jefferson chose Meriwether Lewis to explore the west. He invited his friend William Clark to join him. This was their encampment during the winter of 1805-1806 before they returned east to St. Louis.

Fort Klamath - 1 mile South of Klamath City.

Established 1863 to protect settlers on the western part of Oregon Trail. Abandoned in 1889.

Newport - Yaquina Bay Lighthouse

Built 1871 soon after founding of Newport, Oregon. Captain James Cook made landfall on March 7, 1778. His landfall interested Thomas Jefferson that led to the Louisiana purchase and the Lewis & Clark Expedition.

PENNSYLVANIA

Philadelphia - Independence Hall - 520 Chestnut St.

Built in 1753 as Pennsylvania State House.

Declaration of Independence and United States Constitution were debated and adopted here. Several other historical sites and monuments within walking distance. (Liberty Bell)

Nearby is the Signer Monument dedicated to those who signed their names to these documents.

Philadelphia - Betsy Ross House - 239 Arch St.

Maker of the First Stars and Stripes Flag. She produced flags for the government for over 50 yrs.

Benjamin Franklin's Burial - 340 N. 5th St.

Died 1790 at the age of 84. His accomplishments are too numerous to mention. A true patriot.

Gettysburg - Battle of Gettysburg.

July 1-3, 1863, Gen. Lee meets Gen. Meade in a small town of Gettysburg, PA. One of the best battlefields in the United States.

Farmington - Fort Necessity - National Pike.

Early battle of the French and Indian War, July 3, 1754, which resulted in the surrender of British Forces under Colonel George Washington, age 22. Nearby is grave of British Major General Edward Braddock who died trying to capture French held Fort Duquesne.

Chadds Ford - Brandywine Battlefield

On Sept. 11, 1777, Washington's Army of about 11,000 was defeated by 18,000 British under the command of Howe.

Malvern - Battle of the Clouds.

Washington's encampment after defeat at Brandywine.

Howe pursued, but sudden heavy rain resulted in wet gunpowder for Washington's Troop, so they retreated northwest.

Valley Forge - Washington's Winter Encampment

Washington's Army camped here from Dec. 19, 1777, to June 19, 1778.

Washington made his headquarters in Isaac Potts house.

York - Gen. Horatio Gates Residence - 157 W. Market St.

Was home of Gen. Gates from - 1727-1806. House was connected to the Golden Plough Tavern. Built in 1741

York - Capital of the Nation Sept. 30, 1777, to June 27, 1778

The articles of confederation were adopted here Nov. 15, 1777, with the name - The United States of America

Ligonier - Fort Ligonier - South Market St. Rt. 30

Built 1758 as British fortification from the French and Indian

War. Was never taken in its 8 yrs of existence.

Washington Crossing - Washington Crossing the Delaware

Dec. 25-26, 1776, Washington's Army crosses into Trenton

New Jersey to surprise Hessian Forces.

Shanksville - Flight 93 Memorial - Somerset County

Commemorates the crash of United Flight 93 Sept. 11 attacks only flight of the four hijacked aircraft that did not reach its target. All occupants died including the four terrorists.

SOUTH CAROLINA

Charleston - Fort Sumter

Built to protect Charleston, SC. from naval invasion. The beginning of the Civil War started here.
April 12, 1861

Sullivans Island - Fort Moultrie

Built 1776 for protection of Charleston. Built with palmetto logs inspiring the flag and state nickname "The Palmetto State" Fort was in use till 1947.

Charleston - Old Slave Mart - 6 Chalmers St.

Built in 1859 and was a Slave Auction Facility.

Houses also a Slave Mart Museum.

Mt. Pleasant. - Patriots Point - 40 Patriots Point Rd.

Home to three ships, USS Yorktown, USS Laffey, USS Clamagore View Medal of Honor Museum aboard the Yorktown, 28

Naval Aircraft, and artifacts from other wars.

Pineville - Francis Marion's Grave - Hwy 45

Francis Marion, known as the Swamp Fox, served in the American Revolutionary War. He was a Persistent Adversary of the British. Considered the Father of Guerilla Warfare. He died Feb 27, 1795, at age 63.

Abbeville - Secession Hill - Secession Street

Citizens gathered here Nov. 22, 1860, to adopt ordinance to secede from the Union. One month later South Carolina seceded from the Union.

Cheraw - Henry McIver House - 143 McIver St.

He was signer of Ordinance of Secession, and a Captain in Confederate Cavalry. Gen. William T. Sherman used as his headquarters for several days in March of 1865

Charleston - CS H.L. Hunley - 1250 Supply St.

Submarine of Confederate States of America. First combat submarine to sink a warship, USS Housatonic. Sub and crew were lost before it returned to base

Built in Mobile, AL and launched in July 1863. Was raised in yr. 2000. And is on display.

Ninety-Six - Ninety-Six Historic Site - 1103 SC-248

Nov. 19-21, 1775, the first land battle in South Carolina fortified in 1780 by the British. Major General Nathanael Greene led a siege against Fort but failed to retake the town.

Camden - Battle of Camden - North of Camden

August 16, 1780, British troops under Gen. Cornwallis defeated U.S. Forces of Gen. Horatio Gates.

Blacksburg, - Kings Mountain Military Park - 2625 Park Rd.

Oct. 7, 1780, the left wing of Lord Cornwallis Army was destroyed. Thomas Jefferson viewed Kings Mountain as "The Turning Point" in the war.

Gaffney - Cowpens Battlefield - 4001 Chesnee Hwy.

Brigadier General Daniel Morgan won the battle of Cowpens, over British Lt. Colonel Tarleton, on Jan. 17, 1781

British casualties were estimated at 600 compared to 72 American.

SOUTH DAKOTA

Deadwood - Old West Town - 501 Main St.

Walk the streets where Wild Bill Hickok, Seth Bullock and Calamity Jane walked. 1876 Gold Rush Town.

See Number 10 Saloon where Wild Bill was murdered Aug. 2, 1876

See site where assassin Jack McCall was captured.

Deadwood - Mount Moriah Cemetery

Final resting place of Wild Bill, Calamity Jane and Seth Bullock by tradition the American flag flies over cemetery 24 hrs. a day.

Black Hills - Mt. Theodore Roosevelt Monument

31 ft. stone tower honoring Theodore Roosevelt. Erected by Seth Bullock

Standing Rock Reservation - Sitting Bull Monument - Dec. 15, 1890

Indian Police were sent to arrest Sitting Bull, a gunfight occurred and Sitting Bull was killed. Thus ended the life of a great Lakota leader.

Wounded Knee Creek - Battle of Wounded Knee

Dec. 29, 1890, the U.S. Army massacred nearly 300 Lakota people. The Lakota dead were buried in a mass grave.

Lemmon - Monument to Hugh Glass

Hugh Glass was a fur trapper, a mountain man of the early 19th century. He survived a grizzly bear attack in 1823

He would die 10 yrs later on the Yellowstone River by Arikara Indians. A true mountain man played by Leonardo DiCaprio in the movie "The Revenant"

TENNESSEE

Nashville - The Hermitage - 4580 Rachel's Lane

Andrew Jackson's home which he purchased July 5, 1804

Best preserved early U.S. presidential home.

Columbia - President Polk's Home - W. 7th & High St.

The Eleventh President of the United States lived here in

1816 at the age of 21. Was his home till 1824.

Rutherford - Davy Crockett Cabin - 21219 N. Trenton St.

Cabin restored partly from timbers of his original home. This was Crockett's last home.

His mother is buried here.

Lawrenceburg - Davy Crockett Museum - 1 Public Square

Davy Crockett was a pioneer, soldier, politician and was born near here Aug. 17, 1786

Shiloh - Shiloh Military Park - 1055 Pittsburg Landing Rd.

Battle of Shiloh began April 6-7, 1862, resulting in a six month fight for railroad junction at Corinth

Goodlettsville - Mansker's Station - I-65 North of Nashville

Station was built by Kasper Mansker 1780 Log Fort to protect travelers from Indians.

Hohenwald - Meriwether Lewis Death & Burial Site - Natchez Trace Mile Rd.

38 Site of Grinder House where Lewis met his death Oct. 11, 1809

Memphis - Lorraine Hotel - 450 Mulberry St.

April 4, 1968, Rev. Martin Luther King Jr. was assassinated by James Earl Ray.

Dover - Fort Donelson - 120 Lock D Rd.

Fort built in 1862 and controlled by Confederates till Gen. Grant captured Fort opening two rivers, the Tennessee River and the Cumberland River. First major successes for Union of the War. Remained in Union hands till the end of Civil War.

Dover - Dover Hotel - 101 Petty St.

Built between 1851 and 1853 to accommodate riverboat travelers. General Grant met Gen. Buckner here to discuss Grant's surrender terms.

Clinton - Museum of Appalachia - 2819 Andersonville Hwy.

Living history museum of the people of southern Appalachia. Plenty of artifacts and history here.

TEXAS

San Antonio - Alamo Mission

Feb. 23, - March 6, 1836, William Travis, Davy Crockett and Jim Bowie with about 250 men, died by the hand of Santa Anna and his army. Thus ended the siege of the Alamo.

Victoria - Fannin Battleground Site - 734 FM 2506

Commemorates the Battle of Coleto Creek, fought March 19 and 20 1836 between Col.

Fannin and Mexican General Urrea.

Fannin and his men surrendered and were executed few days later at nearby Presidio La Bahia.

Houston - Battle of Jacinto - Near Todays La. Porte

On April 21, 1836, General Sam Houston defeated Mexican General Santa Anna.

650 Mexicans killed to 11 for Houston's Army. Nearby is the Battleship Texas

Odessa - Chris Kyle Memorial - TX - 191 Frontage Rd.

Memorial to slain Navy Seal and American Sniper Chris Kyle. Kyle was killed in 2013 at a Texas shooting range by former marine.

Waco - Waco Suspension Bridge - 101 N. University Parks Dr.

Opened on Nov. 20, 1869, as toll bridge. No other bridge or ferry could be built within five miles. It contains about 3 million bricks

Texarkana. - James Bowie Statue - 800 State Line Av.

Hero of the Alamo who loved adventure. Bowie County named for him.

Angleton - Stephen F. Austin Statue - S. Walker St.

76-foot-tall statue of one of the founders of Texas.

Justice of the Peace, Law West of the Pecos.

See Jersey Lilly Saloon and Bean Opera House he built in honor of his romance with Singer Lillian Langtry.

Fort Davis - Fort Davis Historic Site - 101 Lt. Flipper Dr.

Established Oct. 1854 to protect travelers on the San Antonio - El Paso, Rd. named for Jefferson Davis who was Secretary of War at the time. - Deactivated in 1891.

Ft. Stockton

Became a city Dec. 27, 1910, after a 56 to 51 vote. Original settlement was St. Gall. Plenty of buildings to view.

Corpus Christi - USS Lexington - 2914 N. Shoreline Blvd.

CV-16 was launched Sept. 23, 1942, nicknamed "The Blue Ghost"

Fredericksburg - Museum of the Pacific War - 340 E. Austin St.

This is the boyhood home of Fleet Admiral Chester W. Nimitz

The museum is in the old Nimitz Hotel and tells the story of Nimitz through his life.

Austin-Lyndon Baines Johnson Library - 2313 Red River St.

Dedicated May 22, 1971, to 36th President of the United States.

Dallas - George W. Bush Presidential Center - 2943 SMU Blvd.

Dedicated April 25, 2013, and will be future resting place of George W. Bush, 43rd President of the United States, and his wife Laura Bush.

College Station - George H.W. Bush Presidential Library - 1000 George Bush Dr. West. Dedicated Nov. 6, 1997, to the 41st President of the United States.

Dallas - Dealey Plaza - City Park West End of Dallas where on Nov. 22, 1963 President John F. Kennedy was assassinated.

Dallas - Clyde Barrow Filling Station - 1221 Singleton Blvd.

Clyde Barrow and his gang visited the residence often.

Lovelady - Eastham Prison - 2665 Prison Rd. 1

Clyde Barrow did time here till his escape Jan. 16, 1934

Barrow wanted revenge on the prison, he loathed.

Huntsville - Sam Houston Statue - 7600 TX-75

Dedicated to Sam Houston, one of the founding fathers of Texas. Leader of Army of Texas during War or Independence from Mexico

Waco - Texas Ranger Hall of Fame - 100 Texas Ranger Trail

Museum of Texas Rangers Law Enforcement Agency.

Greenville - Audie Murphy Museum - 600 I-30 Frontage Rd. 4309

Memorial to Audie Murphy, most decorated soldier of WWII.

Many weapons belonging to him are on display

UTAH

Corinne - Golden Spike Historical Park - 6200 N. 22300 W

May 10, 1869, The Transcontinental Railroad was completed with Leland Stanford driving the 17.6 karat gold spike. Spike is on display at Cantor Arts Center at Stanford University.

Delta - Japanese WWII Internment Camp. - 55 West Main

Opened 1942 as Concentration Camp housing immigrants who had come from Japan. Camp closed Oct. 1945

Circleville - Butch Cassidy Boyhood Home - US 89

Outlaw Butch Cassidy, born Robert Leroy Parker, grew up here.

Wendover - Wendover Air Force Base

Used from 1941-1965 as training base for B-17 and B24 crews.

B-29's who dropped atomic bomb also trained here.

VIRGINIA

Appomattox - Appomattox Court House - 111 National Park Dr.

April 9, 1865, General Lee surrendered his Army of Northern Virginia to General Grants Army of the Potomac. The McLean house was meeting place for surrender.

Bedford - National D-Day Memorial - 3 Overlord Circle

Tribute to sacrifice of allied forces on D-Day June 6, 1944

34 soldiers from Bedford were part of D-Day. Nineteen died on the first day.

Lexington - Lee Chapel - Washington & Lee University

Located inside is statue of Robert E. Lee asleep on the battlefield Gen. Lee is buried beneath the chapel. Lee's horse

"Traveller" is buried just outside the chapel.

Charlottesville - Monticello - 931 Thomas Jefferson Pkwy

Plantation of Thomas Jefferson, the 3rd President of the United States. Beautiful home with plenty of Jefferson artifacts.

Lexington - Stonewall Jackson Home - 8 E Washington St.

Thomas "Stonewall" Jackson lived here from 1858-1861

Petersburg - Petersburg National Battlefield - 5001 Siege Rd.

Civil War Siege of Petersburg 1864-1865. Pennsylvania coal miners burrowed 511 ft., then packed 4 tons of powder under the Confederate Battery. Fuse was lit at 3:15 am. They fell short of their target.

Richmond - Tredegar Iron Works - 470 Tredegar St.

Opened in 1837 was one of the few firms that could make cannon. By wars end, they had made 1,100 cannon

Arlington - Arlington National Cemetery

Final resting place for many, who have given their lives for American freedom

Yorktown - Siege of Yorktown

Last major land battle of the American Revolutionary War

Oct. 19, 1781, British Lt. Gen. Cornwallis was defeated by Continental Army led by General George Washington and French Army Troops led by Comte de Rochambeau.

Norfolk - MacArthur Memorial - 198 Bank St. Memorial

About the life of General Douglas MacArthur

The tomb of General MacArthur and his wife are in the rotunda.

Nine galleries about his life and many artifacts.

Alexandria - Gadsby Tavern - 134 N. Royal St.

Built 1752 was a tavern and hotel. Held here was the first celebration of George Washington's birthday, which he attended. From these steps Washington held his last military review and gave his last military order Nov. 1799

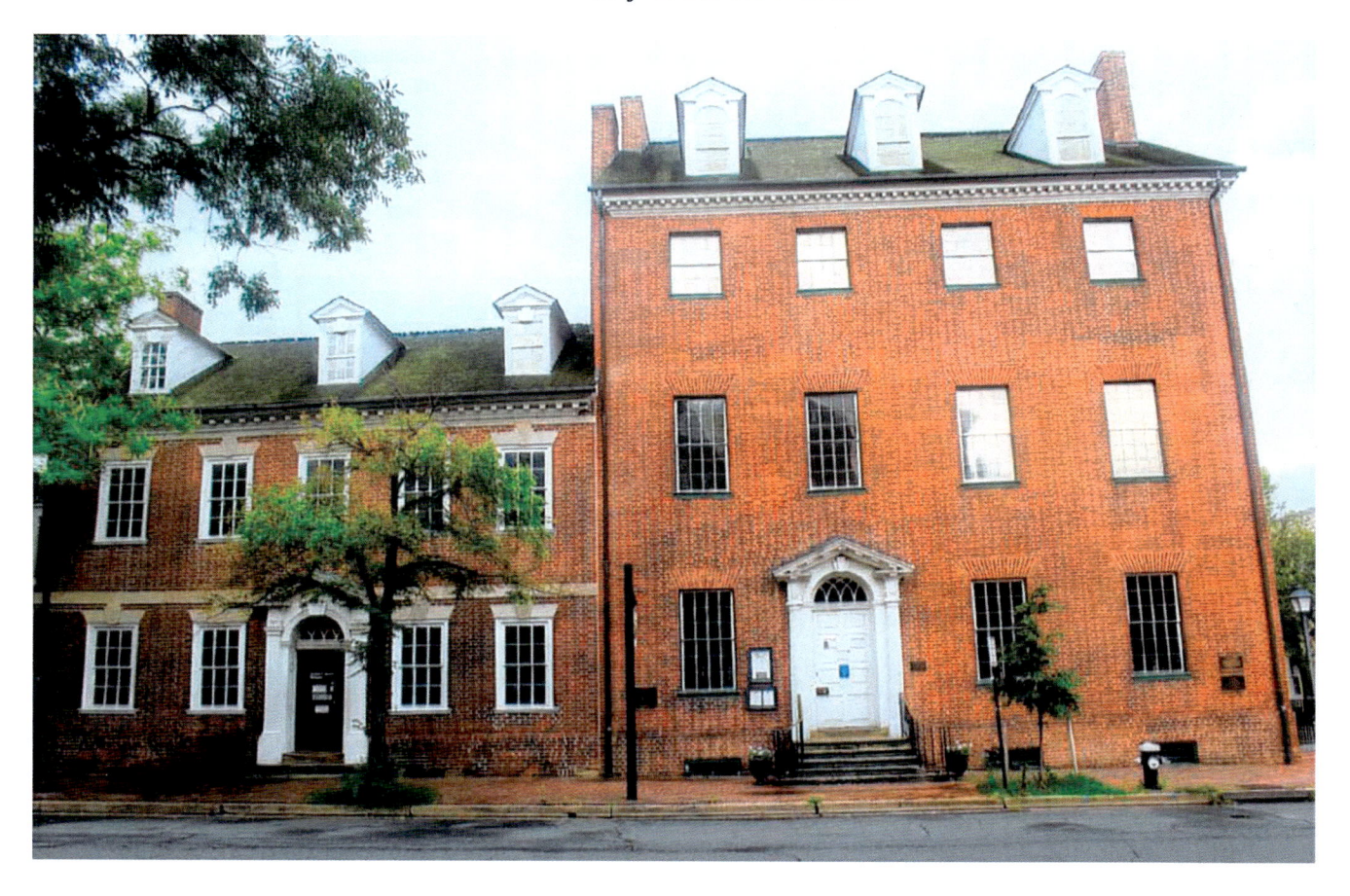

Richmond - White House of the Confederacy - 1201 E. Clay St.

Built in 1818 this was the Executive Mansion of President

Jefferson Davis and his family 1861-1865.

Chantilly - Steven F. Udar - Hazy Center - 14390 Air and Space

Museum Pkwy National Air and Space Museum.

Exhibits include Discovery Space Shuttle, The Enola Gay, Gemini 7 Space Capsule, SR-71 Blackbird

Mount Vernon - George Washington's Estate - 3200 Mt. Vernon Memorial Hwy.

Plantation of George Washington, the First President of the United States and his wife Martha.

Montpelier Station - James Madison Home - 11350 Constitution Hwy

James Madison, the Fourth President of the United States and his wife Dolley resided on this plantation.

Charlottesville - Michie Tavern - 683 Thomas Jefferson Pkwy.

Established in 1784, served as a meeting place and provided food, drink and lodging.

Winchester - Home of Daniel Morgan - 226 Amherst St.

General Daniel Morgan lived here till his death July 6, 1802. His daughter then took over ownership. A summary of Morgan's life can be seen at 304 East Piccadilly St.

Hopewell - Grant's Headquarters at City Point - 1001 Pecan Av.

Was port on the James River during the last days of the Civil War. From the port, the railroad supported Union Forces during the siege of Petersburg. President Lincoln spent 3 weeks at City Point April 1865. I'm sure Gen. Grant and President Lincoln had much to talk about.

Jamestown - First Permanent English Settlement in the Americas.

Established May 14, 1607, and served as Colonial Capital from 1616 to 1699

More than 80% of the colonist died in 1609-1610 from starvation and disease. In August 1619 the first slaves arrived from Africa.

Charles City - Berkeley Plantation - 12602 Harrison Landing Rd.

Built 1726 was one of the first plantations in America. Benjamin Harrison, signer of the Declaration of Independence lived here. His son, William Henry Harrison,

9th President of the United States was born here 1773. General McClellan had his headquarters here while the Army of the Potomac was near.

Lorton - George Washington Gristmill - 5512 Mt. Vernon Memorial Hwy.

Built in 1770 as part of the Mount Vernon Plantation. Used to produce flour and cornmeal for the plantation. He later added a distillery operation.

Port Royal - John Wilkes Booth Capture - Rt. 301 2 miles N. of Port Royal.

Foundation of house can be found by walking into the woods.

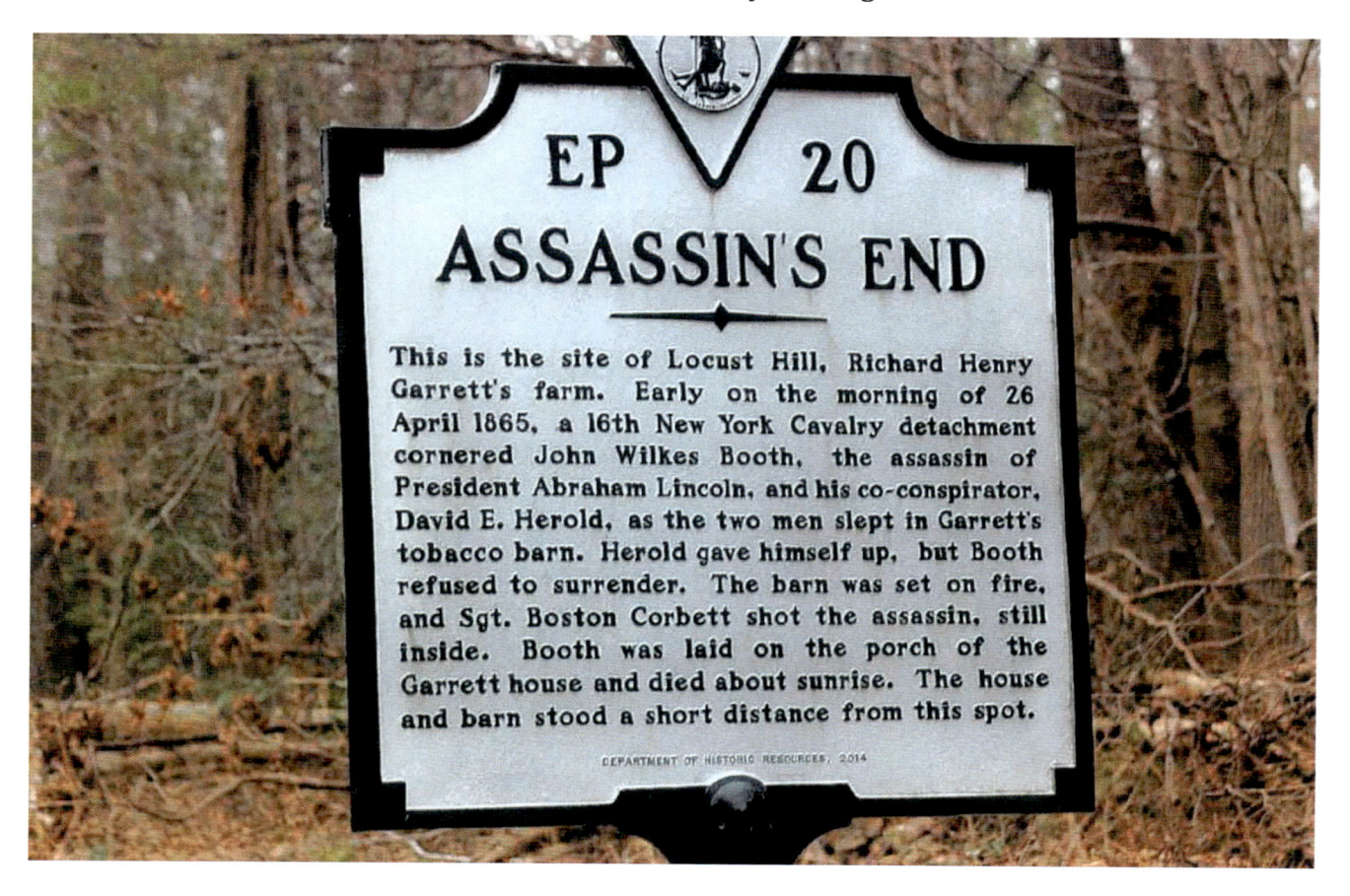

Bull Run - First Major Battle of Civil War.

July 21, 1861, 30 miles west of Washington, DC. Confederate

Forces defeated 18,000 poorly trained Union Army.

Staunton - Woodrow Wilson Library - 20 N. Coalter St.

Contains the birthplace of the 28th President of the United States and his life, 1856-1924

Woodford - Stonewall Jackson Death Site - 12019 Stonewall Jackson Rd.

Jackson spent the final 6 days of his life on Thomas C. Chandler's plantation.

Fredericksburg - Battlefield - 1013 Lafayette Blvd.

Civil War battle of Fredericksburg fought Dec. 11-15 1862

Remembered as one of the most one-sided battles of the war. Union casualties more than doubled the Confederate loses.

New Market - Battlefield - 8895 George Collins Pkwy

Civil War Battle fought May 15, 1864. This battle included cadets from Virginia Military Institute (VMI) which resulted in the Confederate's defeating the Union Army.

Charles City - Shirley Plantation - 501 Shirley Plantation Rd.

Built 1723 and is the oldest active plantation in Virginia, and the oldest family owned business in North America, dating back to 1614.

WASHINGTON

Mount St. Helens - Cascade Range

May 18, 1980 major eruption, the most deadly eruption in U.S. history. View from Visitor. Center is amazing.

WEST VIRGINIA

Parkersburg - Blennerhassett Island - Wood County, Ohio River

Ride a paddlewheel boat to get to island. Aaron Burr and Harman Blennerhassett are alleged to have plotted treason against the United States.

Charles Town - John Brown Trial - 100 E. Washington St.

Oct. 16, 1859 abolitionist John Brown and his followers attacked the Harpers Ferry Arsenal. They were captured and put on trial in the Charles Town Courthouse. They were found guilty and were hung Dec. 2, 1859.

Mineral County - Nancy Hanks Birthplace - Rt. 50

Birthplace of Nancy Hanks, Abe Lincoln's mother born 1782, died 1818 from milk sickness.

Buckhannon - Pringle Tree - Pringle Tree Park Rd. US. 119

The Pringle brothers John and Samuel lived in the hollow of a Sycamore tree 1760's. They were first settlers in this area. They lived here for 3 yrs. after fleeing from Fort Pitt.

Berkeley Springs - Berkeley Springs - 127 Fairfax St.

`See George Washington's bathtub 1748. He was a surveyor's assistant at age 16, and he enjoyed the 72-degree bathing experience.

Pt. Pleasant - Mothman Statue - 201 4th St.

Statue depicting the "Mothman" creature of Pt. Pleasant. Silver Bridge collapse is part of the legend made popular by Richard Gere movie. Abandoned Army Igloo Ammo Bunker nearby is point where they believed he stayed. Legend remains a mystery today.

Harper's Ferry - John Brown's Fort - Shenandoah & Potomac St.

Built in 1848 as a fire engine house. John Brown and his followers sought refuge here during their raid on the armory.

Harper's Ferry - Jefferson Rock

Thomas Jefferson on a visit to Harper's Ferry in 1783. Where the Shenandoah meets the Potomac, Jefferson said "This scene is worth a voyage across the Atlantic."

Bunker Hill - Col. Morgan Morgan - Winchester Av. Rt. 11

American pioneer who was among the earliest persons to settle in present day West Virginia around 1732. His cabin is located 3.5 miles west of Rt. 11. He also established Christ Church in 1740. He is buried in the cemetery, along with Morgan Morgan II

Martinsburg - B & O Railroad Roundhouse - 100 E. Liberty St.

Built around 1842 and burned by Confederates. Rebuilt in
1866, and East Roundhouse was built in 1872.

Omar - Hatfield Cemetery - Access Rd. WV 44

Anderson "Devil Anse" Hatfield 1839-1921 is buried here atop a steep hill. Was leader of the Hatfield clan during the feud with the McCoys.

A life size statue, imported from Italy marks his grave.

Ronceverte - Organ Cave - 242 Organ Cave Dr.

Known for Saltpeter before 1835. During Civil War was a source of powder for General Lee's army. General Lee also held church services for his troops in the cave.

White Sulphur Springs - The Greenbrier - 101 W. Main St.

A resort that has been welcoming guest since 1778. In 1958-1961, under the Eisenhower Administration, construction began on a underground bunker to keep our government operating if ever attack by nuclear weapons. It was never used and was kept a secret for over 30 years.

Williamstown - Henderson Hall - 517 Old River Rd.

Built 1836, Italianate style, features original furnishings from the

1700's to the oil boom days of the 20th century. 8,000 square feet, with 16 rooms, was centerpiece of 2600 acre plantation.

Martinsburg - Belle Boyd House - 126 E. Race St.

Built in 1853 by Ben Boyd, father of Isabella (Belle) Boyd a Confederate spy and friend of Gen. Stonewall Jackson. After the war, she married a Union officer.

WISCONSIN

Ripon - Birthplace of Republican Party - 303 Blackburn St.

School house on March 20, 1854 was held first meeting to break free from old parties an form the Republican Party.

Victory - Battle of Bad Axe

Just road side markers for battle that took place between Sauk and Fox Indians and the U.S. Army on August 1-2 1832. Final battle of Black Hawk War. Indians trying to flee across the Mississippi were massacred.

WYOMING

Ft. Bridger - State Historical Site

Established in 1842. Resupply point for wagons on the Oregon Trail, California Trail and Mormon Trail

Fort was last stop for Donner Party. Closed in 1890

Laramie - Wyoming Territorial Prison - 975 Snowy Range Rd.

Built in 1872, and is one of the oldest buildings in Wyoming, was federal prison from 1872 to 1890. Butch Cassidy was inmate. Near Laramie you can still see wagon ruts of Oregon Trail.

Laramie - Fort Laramie - 965 Grey Rocks Rd.

Built 1834 as military installation at the confluence of the Laramie and North Platte rivers. See memorial to greatest ride in history. Horse ridden by John Phillips on Dec. 24-25 1866 seeking aid for Fort Kearny. Horse went 236 miles in two days, through a blizzard with temperature below zero. Horse died from exhaustion after arriving at Fort Laramie.

Cody - Buffalo Bill Center of the West - 720 Sheridan Av.

Five museums featuring artifacts and art of the American West. The best museum of the west

Buford - Ames Brothers Historic Site - 210 Monument Rd.

Memorial to the Ames brothers, Oliver and Oakes for their contributions in building of the Transcontinental Railroad. Monument is located

near the highest elevation of the railroad route 8,247 ft.

Barnum-Hole-in-the-Wall - I-25N to Rt. 190 West look for signs

Butch Cassidy's wild bunch met at a log cabin here. Cabin is preserved at Old Trail Town Museum in Cody.

Laramie - Abraham Lincoln Memorial Monument - 136 US Service Rd. 705A

12½ ft. bust of Lincoln resting on granite pedestal at summit rest area east of Laramie on I-80. "That there should be a Lincoln Highway across this country is an important thing" Henry B. Joy First President of Lincoln Highway Association.

Alcova - Independence Rock Rt 220

Large granite rock used as landmark on the Oregon, Mormon, and California emigrant trails.

Made in United States
Orlando, FL
05 April 2024

45489103R00062